HAWAII ISLAND ARTISTS
AND FRIENDS OF THE ARTS

HAWAII ISLAND ARTISTS
AND FRIENDS OF THE ARTS

second edition

edited by Jerré E. Tanner

Malama Arts Inc.
Kailua-Kona, Hawaii 1990

edited by Jerré E. Tanner
designed by John Thomas

assistant editor Janet L. Coburn

community liaisons Janet L. Coburn
Laura Lewis, Christy Akiona

No part of this book may be reproduced, stored in a retrieval system or transmitted in any form or by means electronic, mechanical, photocopying, recording or otherwise, without prior permission from Malama Arts Inc. Brief text quotations for book review purposes are exempted.

All Hawaii telephone numbers which appear in this book have an area code of (808).

© Malama Arts Inc., 1990
all rights reserved

"Henry Weeks
Kona's Master Woodworker"
© Rebecca Crockett, 1990
all rights reserved

"Hualalai"
© Ray Freed, 1990, all rights reserved

© All artwork is copyrighted by the artist/creator unless otherwise stated.
All rights to the individual artworks are strictly reserved by the artist.

a publication of
Malama Arts Inc.
Post Office Box 1478
Kailua-Kona, Hawaii 96745
phone 329-5828

Post Office Box 1761
Honolulu, Hawaii 96806

ISBN: 0-931909-07-4

printed in British Hong Kong

CONTENTS

8   Foreword
       Jerré E. Tanner

13   Album of Color Plates
      Featured Artists

66   Featured Artists Information

70   Artist Benefactors

78   Hawaii's Heritage
      Henry Weeks
      Kona's Master Woodworker
      Rebecca Crockett

84   Cover Artists

86   Galleries

93   Art Centers

108 Friends of the Arts

114 Artists Index

124 Index

FOREWORD

The second edition of *Hawaii Island Artists and Friends of the Arts* continues and expands the ideas accomplished in the premiere edition. The impact of the premiere edition on our political, business and arts community has been considerable, if we are to judge by the praise it has already enjoyed. Indeed, the book's influence has been greater in some areas than we imagined. It has provided a new and persuasive tool for those who promote our Island abroad. One of our artist's benefactors took the book to Japan as gifts to his business associates. Malama Arts has received orders for books as far west as Australia and as far east as Nova Scotia. The book's designer, artist John Thomas, and I attended the 1990 opening of the State Legislature and handed out books to the legislators, introducing them to our Island's artists. They were universally impressed with the high quality and diversity of those artists featured.

As it turns out, the premiere edition tended to be classical in its design, whereas the second edition lent itself to a more experimental approach. Like all pioneer efforts the second edition, as it took shape, required changes in some sections, expansion in others and the addition of a new color section. The Album of Color Plates was expanded to include forty-five artists. One artist, Lloyd Sexton, had sent us a splendidly evocative biography from which we were to glean material for his entry in the book. When the word came of his death on March 23, 1990 the staff and I felt there should be a tribute to his life and work, so we decided to expand his feature to allow printing his essay as the artist's own testament. The Art Centers portion of the book has been expanded to profile six additional not-for-profit art institutions. Each edition of the book will feature a more in-depth profile of the activities of one of the art centers. This year the University of Hawaii at Hilo Campus Center was chosen for special recognition. Concern for 'The Gallery,' an important link in the arts industry, led to the creation of a new section devoted to those galleries with a strong commitment to Hawaii Island Artists. Our poet in the premiere edition, Harvey Hess, and I chose Ray Freed's *Hualalai* from dozens of fine submittals. We hope to continue this tradition in future editions.

Patronage for the artists in the second edition was sought in the same manner as in the first -- from cultured individuals and business leaders. Over fifty percent of the benefactors from the premiere edition continued into the second edition, giving encouragement and support to our artists. Over the last three decades the 'Corporate Collection' gave a much needed financial boost to the arts, and there is every reason to believe that this will continue; however, the new trend for business sponsorship appears to be a mutually beneficial arrangement where the arts will enhance the business image and lend 'class' to their products. Business and art forming a complimentary relationship is the way of the future, according to the authors of *Megatrends 2000*.

The second edition continues to offer an overview of the Island's artistic talents by including woven *hala*, feather *leis*, pottery, fiber wall constructions, ceramic sculpture, bowls, furniture, musical instruments, photography, quilts, art glass and paintings in oil, watercolor and acrylic.

Following the Malama Arts tradition of using a colorful and decorative detail of an artwork on soft cover books, this year's cover is a detail from a ceramic pot, *Fire Birds in a Forest*, by Hilo/Waimea artist Fumie Bonk. This work of art is reproduced in full on the book's inside cover and on page 84. All previous cover artists will continue to have an artwork reproduced in succeeding editions.

Besides focusing on a number of the Island's outstanding contemporary artists in color reproductions and profiles, we have included an artist from the past whose historical significance to our culture is featured in an essay written by an outstanding historian. For the second edition the Kona master woodworker Henry Weeks was chosen. This artist recognized the beauty inherent in the abundant stands of hardwood trees growing on the mountain slopes of our island and early on established a tradition of using wood as a medium for creating art. As evidenced by the fine examples in the premiere and second editions, this tradition is continuing vigorously today. The essay on Henry Weeks is written by Hawaii Island writer Rebecca Crockett. It is our hope that these historical essays will lead many readers to rediscover our Island's artistic heritage.

We abided by the previous editorial decision to give as much space as possible on each page to the color reproduction of the featured artists' work as the art expresses most clearly the artist's intention. This meant there was often little space left for providing supportive information about the artist. The Featured Artist Index was created to provide this ancillary information. A careful reading will provide substantial background on the diverse lives and education of the many artists featured.

The number of artists listed in the final section of the book, the Artists Index, has grown from 283 to 359. This increase reflects some previously overlooked artists, but it also reflects an influx of new artists to Hawaii Island. These new citizens bring with them a rich resource of creative talent and education, adding nourishment to an already flourishing arts community. The arts industry needs to keep pace with the rapid growth of talent. In order for the arts industry to grow it needs support from all strata of our society. For galleries to prosper and perform their vital role in this industry, serious art collectors are needed -- those individuals who have educated themselves to understand, recognize and purchase those works of art which truly capture Significant Form. The industry as a whole needs to be acknowledged and taken seriously by those with official capacity to bring about change. Our government must recognize the importance of the arts in enriching our daily lives and also the value in dollars that the arts industry contributes to the economic well-being of the County and State. The travel industry is already coming to realize that the sophisticated world traveler increasingly demands a rich indigenous culture to supplement the attractions of a beautiful natural environment.

Compiling the second edition has brought fresh insights and has affirmed my belief in the quality of our artists and their determined search for value. At the end of my foreword in the premiere edition I posed a question concerning direction, "Where will all this take us?" I can state with assurance that the visual arts are in better shape today than they were two years ago when we were planning our first edition of this series of books. There are more people devoted to working together. Concerned Islanders are looking for and cultivating those elements in the community which strengthen and unify. A new urgency to 'make it work' has emerged. Manifestations of that direction are two collaborations which appear in this edition. Gary Soukup and David Anderson have combined their talents to create a *tour de force* of six kinds of woods making a symbol of meditation and literary creation. Terrie Rodman and I have combined weaving and music in an alliance which reveals the bonds of both art forms. I look forward to more collaboration in the future. After all, this book itself is a collaboration.

--Jerré E. Tanner, Editor
Kailua-Kona, Hawaii

GOVERNOR'S MESSAGE

Hawaii's superb natural environment, marked by spectacular vistas, cool green mountains, sparkling seashores and clear skies, is often inspiration for Hawaii's artists. Of equal importance are Hawaii's people, a diverse ethnic and cultural mixture, all living together in harmony.

Hawaii Island Artists and Friends of the Arts brings together fine examples of works of those whose creativity celebrates Hawaii.

Congratulations to the artists whose works are displayed in this second volume and to Malama Arts for publishing the series.

Aloha,
John Waihee
GOVERNOR, STATE OF HAWAII

CHAIRMAN'S MESSAGE

Hawaii's distinctive and successful arts climate is largely due to strong public and private support as well as its rich multi-cultural heritage. Along with the natural beauty and historical richness of our island state, the arts have had a healthy setting in which to thrive and do well.

Collections such as *Hawaii Island Artists and Friends of the Arts* benefit all of us -- artist and patron, resident and visitor. It boasts of the variety of talent and the strength of identity we all share in Hawaii.

The Island of Hawaii in particular, is like no other in its depth and breadth of spirit and community. It is deserving of this collection of its diverse arts community and its many supporters. Our appreciation to Malama Arts Inc. for this very fine effort to further extend the arts in Hawaii.

Aloha,
Millicent Kim
CHAIRMAN, STATE FOUNDATION ON CULTURE AND THE ARTS

HUALALAI

Fading sun slants a line
across verdant Hualalai,
greens made brighter
by that last gasp of light,
and the lava land Keahole
slips away like a dark sea wave.

Who knows what trickery startled
the owl Pueo off the road
to perch on the street lamp
as we drove down the darkened drive

or what trickeries coax the gecko to cling
to the ceiling above me now,
mouthing a song like far-off laughter.
He makes it out of air.

by Ray Freed

ALBUM OF COLOR PLATES

Artist Benefactors

The Honolulu Advertiser
Mauna Kea Beach Hotel

Bradley Properties, Ltd.
Putman and Lisa Clark

Alfredo's Photo Studio
Art Mart of Kona
Blackwell Custom Furniture
C. J. Kimberly Realtors
Fiberarts/Topstitch
Holualoa Development Company
HPM Building Supply
Keauhou Beach Hotel
Kona Ranch House
Loyd's Art Supply

Ad Studio Kona
Friends of Garron Alexander
Hawaii Tribune-Herald
Kai Markell, III
Keauhou-Kona Realty, Inc.

Mauna Lani Resort, Inc.
University of Hawaii at Hilo

Hilo Accident & Industrial Injury Clinic
Lanihau Center

Malama Arts Inc.
Maryl Development
Multi-Arts Incorporated
Orchid Isle Auto Center
Peggy Chesnut & Company
Personal Business Manager
Phyllis Sellens and Company
Upcountry Quilters
Winkler Wood Products, Inc.

Keauhou Village Book Shop
Meadow Gold Dairies
Reyn Spooner Inc.
Waimea General Store
William and Kathleen Jardine

LLOYD SEXTON
1912 - 1990

"My hope is that I may have years ahead to create many subjects that are as yet unaccomplished."

-- LLOYD SEXTON

We at Mauna Kea Beach Hotel pay tribute to the late Lloyd Sexton for his fine contribution to the arts of Hawaii. Our guests, visitors and staff alike have long enjoyed his oil paintings of native Hawaiian flowers on display in a conference room named the Lloyd Sexton Gallery. Lithographed prints of these impressive oils were created in Paris in the early 1960s exclusively for Mauna Kea. Laurance S. Rockefeller had the original plates destroyed, and the fine prints have now become valuable limited editions. Though we no longer have the artist with us, his art continues to enrich our lives.

-- ADI KOHLER
President and General Manager

On March 24, 1912 I was born Leo Lloyd Sexton, Jr. in Hilo, Hawaii. I am a great grandson of William and Mary Rice who came to Hawaii from Boston as missionaries on the sailing ship Gloucester in 1840. I am one of the fourth generation of the family to live in the Hawaiian Islands.

My first recollection of an interest in painting was in kindergarten taught by a Mrs. Dranga [Helen Thomas Dranga, see *premiere edition*, page 64-ED] who was a very fine artist painting in a manner not unlike an impressionist. At the early age of five her work had a great appeal for me. When I started grammar school in a one room building called "Mrs. Daly's School", my interest in painting was rekindled through our teacher, an English woman. Though a disciplinarian, she allowed her students to devote time for art. This included copying still life paintings with color crayons. My first attempt was to copy a painting of cherries in a green china bowl.

In high school, my drawings began to appear in my text books. A good grade in biology was due to my carefully rendered drawings, including cross sections, of flowers and plants. During these years I did a good amount of landscape painting, having been introduced to the medium of oil by our librarian Sylvia Charlock who was also an accomplished artist. It was then that I became interested in painting *plein-air*. This led to painting flowers in their settings. Our Hawaiian landscapes lend themselves to romantic backgrounds for our native flowers. I was always interested in the unusual forms of our exotic flowers and their beautiful colors. I began to enlarge my subjects to emphasize their forms; but, unlike Georgia O'Keef, I placed them in a setting in which they would grow.

In 1929 I entered Punahou School in Honolulu as a junior. The closest thing to an art class was the mechanical drawing class, so I continued painting on my own. I did a stage set for one of the plays and cartoons for the annual year book. Shortly after I had graduated from Punahou I had the good fortune to meet Dr. Hoffman from Boston. He admired my work, thought I had sufficient talent to pursue my learning in serious study and recommended the School of the Museum of Fine Arts in Boston. I entered the Museum School in 1931 and became most interested in the design course given by a Miss Ethel Williams from New York. There was a course in life drawing given by two excellent draftsmen, graduates of the Slade School in London. I drew from plaster casts and then from the live model.

During the summer in Hawaii, after the first year at the Museum School, I managed to produce enough paintings for a one man show which was given me in 1932 at the Robert C. Vose Galleries, then on Boylston Street, Boston. The show was comprised of oils of enlarged Hawaiian flowers and pastels of flowers in a still life. A bank holiday was declared the day my show opened. That, coupled with the fact that I was an unknown, resulted in no sales.

In 1933 I was given a one man show at the Honolulu Academy of Arts and then at S. & G. Gumps in San Francisco. My subjects again were florals. Later that year, a painting of mine was entered in the Boston Art Club annual exhibition. I also was pleased to sell three floral textile designs to Arthur Lee & Son in New York. In 1934 I received the Charles Amos Cummings European Traveling Scholarship.

After leaving the museum school I worked in Hilo, Hawaii until the fall of 1935 during which time I was asked by N. W. Ayer & Son to do a painting for a product advertisement for Dole Pineapple Co. Working with our Hawaiian motifs held a fascination for me. This eventually led to a series of paintings for the Dole Pineapple Co., one of which received the New York Art Directors Association Award for best painting in mass magazines.

In September I set out for London and my studies at the Slade School, London University College. The stage design course attracted my interest. It was well presented by a Mr. Polunin and was exciting for a period of time. Then I became interested in figure drawing. Thereafter, most of my time at the Slade School was spent in the figure drawing and portrait classes. I worked very diligently and long hours every day and spent a great deal of time studying the drawings of the European masters, particularly the English portraits which I admired.

In 1936 I submitted an oil painting to the Royal Academy. It was accepted. The subject was an enlarged flower in a Hawaiian setting size 30" by 30". Later that year the same painting was exhibited by invitation at the Russel-Cotes Art Gallery in Bournemouth. A description of the painting in their bulletin read, "We must, in conformity with modern critical trends, single out the most daring of flower studies with the title 'Awa Puhi'. It appears to be some gigantic blossom which, if omnivorous, might engulf a full-sized rat. Lloyd Sexton has given us a vivid, highly finished and strong three dimensional study." At the end of the school year in 1937 I received first prize in figure drawing.

Returning to Hilo I commenced working with Hawaiian subjects again. My immediate goal was to submit a figure painting to the Royal Academy in hopes that it would be accepted. To my delight it was 'hung on the line' and received good reports. My work began to include portrait commissions which seemed to occupy most of the ensuing months until the second World War was upon us. Almost immediately I found myself engaged in camouflage work under the U.S. Engineers, later being sent from Honolulu to manage a plant on the Island of Hawaii. It was another experience using color and form. The medium was chicken wire and dyed burlap garlands. I was the designer and the colorist, and our Hawaiian lei-maker women did the weaving. On March 7, 1942, shortly after the start of the war, I was fortunate to marry Eleanor Wishard.

After the war ended we moved to the Volcano area on the Island of Hawaii and it was there that our daughter Mary Emily was born in 1946. By then I had set up my studio above the garage of a tin-roofed home which we rented for a song from our dear friend Auntie Annabelle Ruddle. Once again I began devoting all my time to painting. The Island of Hawaii offered many landscape subjects with interesting moods.

Oil painting has become my choice of medium over the years. I have always followed a rather traditional manner or style of painting and am influenced by the French Impressionists. Though it may appear so, I do not like copying nature but altering elements of a scene to develop a good composition in the employment of color, form, and lighting. I think quite abstractly in planning a composition. I try to achieve a mood in a landscape and strive for a feeling of light. Our Hawaiian clouds are so beautiful and become an important part in any of my paintings. They are also the most difficult part of a painting for me to render. Some of the commissioned portraits include two governors of Hawaii, a portrait of Princess Ka'iulani for the Ka'iulani Hotel in Honolulu, and Prince Champacak, Barbara Hutton's last husband, Dr. George Straub, Mrs. Lurline Roth, University of Hawaii President Dr. Sinclair, Mr. & Mrs. H. P. Baldwin, Mr. Sam Baldwin, Senator Charles Rice, and Chief Justice Phillip Rice.

In 1957 my one man show at Grossman-Moody in Honolulu received a favorable review by art critic Austin Faricy. In 1961 critic Clare Loring said about my one man show at the Gallery, Hilton Hawaiian Village, "These are representational paintings, but the artist's great concern for light and the qualities of color which can be achieved with light whether it be the transparency of the early morning, the full mellowness of midday, or the deepening mystery in the light of the evening, lifts them into a very personal statement. Sexton says he searches out subject matter forms which are meaningful to him, but feels free to organize the forms creatively to satisfy compositional needs. 'After the Wave' is one of the strongest paintings in the show. The luminosity which envelops the bare and twisted tree resting on the quiet sand bar gives a haunting feeling of eternity. The forms are strongly realized and well composed. The shapes of the clouds repeated by those of the limped pools. Somewhat deeper in color is 'Tree Silhouettes' a painting of a stand of Lehua trees bared of all the foliage by the lava flow still molten below them. The softly lit tracery pattern of the trunks and branches is caught into the mystery of the vibrant blue of the evening sky."

In 1964 I did a series of enlarged flower paintings in oil for the Mauna Kea Beach Hotel on the Island of Hawaii from which lithographs were done in the *atelier* of Mourlot in Paris. In 1965 I became a member of the Grand Central Art Gallery in New York. My paintings have been entered in group shows there. This same year a landscape painting of mine was shown at the New York World's Fair in the Hawaiian Exhibit.

The Contemporary Art Center in Honolulu favored me with a one man show in 1966. I shall forever be most grateful for the kind words Jean Charlot used in a critique of my show. The review read, "Lloyd Sexton is an excellent conservative painter, a rarity in our days. In the good old times it was valid approval to remark of a painted portrait 'if it could only talk!' Of Sexton's landscapes it could innocently be said that they are nature itself. A well-staged play can communicate the vividness of actual events. Sexton's nature is such a well-directed play. The clouds that cast fleeting shadows on mountain slopes have been arrested in their gliding motion at the instant of maximum effect. The sun that lights the *kukui* groves in the hollow cliffs has been stopped in it's course by this Modern Joshua.

"Sexton believes that intelligence is on a par with sensitivity in art-making. Craft of a high order is needed to put on canvas the glissandos from light to dark and from hue to hue. Never is a color used at it's primary strength unless it be an electric blue that Sexton favors as a foil to the delicacy of his color blends. I singled out '*Mountain Shapes*' for its sculpturesque monumentality. '*Queen's Bath*' features the cubic shapes of black rocks bathed in an aura of spirituality. Here Sexton reaches further than patient craft, towards certain realms of art that may be felt but cannot be analyzed."

In 1968 Eastern Airlines organized a group show of artist paintings in Hawaii. Juliet May Frazer wrote of my entry '*Awakening,*' "... Here Sexton's meticulous realism creates a haunting surrealism."

For whatever it means, I was a past president of the Hawaii Painters & Sculptors League. My paintings have been hung in group shows in Honolulu, San Francisco, Oakland, Boston, New York and London. In 1975 my biography was entered in *International Who's Who in Art and Antiques* and later in *Who's Who in the West*.

My hope is that I may have years ahead to create many subjects that are as yet unaccomplished.

-- LLOYD SEXTON
assisted by his daughter
Mary Emily Sexton Greenwell
Honolulu, Hawaii, May 8, 1989

sponsored by MAUNA KEA BEACH HOTEL

above
KALAUPAPA SHORELINE
oil on stretched linen canvas
18 by 24 inches
collection of Mrs. Lloyd Sexton
photograph by Gordon Ng

right
LLOYD SEXTON IN HIS STUDIO
portrait photograph by
Mary Emily Sexton Greenwell

DAVID GOMES

David Gomes, born in Kohala on Hawaii Island, grew up listening to *luau* music. His father, Franklin P. Gomes, taught David music as a child. David got his first guitar when he was thirteen. He was introduced to classical flamenco by a Hawaii Preparatory Academy teacher named Robert Mitchell. While attending University of Santa Clara he studied with Mariano Cordoba in Palo Alto. In 1972 David went to Spain to study flamenco guitar in Madrid with Juan "Triguito" Gonsalez and returned two years later to study with Maria Sanchez Cortez. In Madrid he met guitar maker Paulino Bernabe and started to make guitars. Moving back to Kohala in 1975 David began to build his own guitars and ukuleles. He also continued to play guitar and appear regularly at Kohala Coast resorts. Each instrument takes over three weeks to make. David is constantly refining his techniques and tools creating what he needs to make the instrument. David makes his home in Kohala with his wife, Maurine, and their two children.

opposite right
TENOR UKULELE
body: curly koa
neck: Honduras mahogany
bridge and fret board: ebony
purfling: rosewood and maple, abalone inlay
27 inches long
collection of Maurine Gomes
photograph by Alfredo Furelos
portrait photograph by Alfredo Furelos

sponsored by MAUNA LANI RESORT, INC.

Raindrops on a taro leaf in remote Waipi'o Valley: luminous, like liquid crystal, and as pure and sacred as water given by the gods. Photographer Franco Salmoiraghi captures these qualities in a single photograph, "Wai'apo" [see premiere edition, pages 56 and 57--ED], his signature image and one of his many tributes to the vast mysteries of nature. The sacred and the sensuous are one and the same in his vision. With a keen intuition he detects and captures with

FRANCO SALMOIRAGHI

his camera the spiritual essence of nature, people, places, and moments, each photograph a clear and reverent poem of all that cannot be said in words. For 20 years he has tapped the creative vigor of the Big Island and embraced its awesome power. The late kumu hula Edith Kanaka'ole, the ancient footsteps of Waipi'o Valley, the pristine snows of Mauna Kea, the roiling eruption of a volcano -- in capturing on film these inspired moments he has also charted the changes of a very special place and its people. He was a teacher of photography at the University of Hawaii and today is one of Hawaii's most respected and versatile photographers. An award-winning photojournalist, he is also a fine art, documentary, commercial, and portrait photographer

sponsored by THE HONOLULU ADVERTISER

whose work has been shown and collected extensively. More than 20 of Franco's works have been purchased by the Hawaii State Foundation on Culture and the Arts. Franco is also well known for his contributions to the major magazines of Hawaii and Asia. He was a contributing photographer for the book *Kahala*, which won a Communication Arts award; the *Apa Insight Guide on Hawaii*; *A Day in the Life of Hawaii*; and a book on Thailand called *Seven Days in the Kingdom*. Among his most significant published works is the book *Christmas Island* which won a 1989 Lowell Thomas Award from the Society of American Travel Writers in the travel book category. His fine art photography also appears exclusively in *Change We Must*. In this fine book, Franco's black-and-white photographs complement the extraordinary story of Hawaiian kupuna and metaphysician Nana Veary in her lifelong spiritual journey. Franco exhibits at the Volcano Art Center, Gallery of Great Things in Waimea and at Gallery for Fine Photography (New Orleans).

above
LEVITATION
photography, toned silver print
9 by 13 inches

text by Jocelyn Fujii
portrait photograph by Renee Iijima

In 1987 the State Foundation on Culture and the Arts selected Tsugi Kaiama as a Master Lei Maker. Her work was also displayed at the Academy of Art in Honolulu during the celebration of Paniolo folk art. Tsugi was invited to participate in the Smithsonian Institution's Folklife program in Washington, D. C. In 1990 she exhibited leis and broaches in Malama Arts' Invitational Exhibition at Wailoa Center, Hilo. Tsugi has made feather lei for more than 50 years. When asked what has inspired her to continue making feather lei she said she got great pleasure from making something so beautiful out of natural materials. All her designs are original. She makes lei for family and for a list of distinguished clients. Her large family provides her with pelts from their hunting expeditions. Using the feathers for feather lei insured that little was wasted of the game birds. During World War II large expeditions of visiting army officers were taken game bird hunting on the Parker Ranch lands. The birds were brought to Tsugi who remembers doing a lot of skinning during the war years. Tsugi is represented by Kaiama Featherwork.

TSUGI KAIAMA

opposite right
FEATHERWORK, LEI AND BROACHES
lei (l. to r.) wild turkey and peacock; kaleej and peacock; pheasant; pheasant broach - pheasant; owl broach - erckel
collection of the artist
photograph by Alfredo Furelos
portrait photograph by Alfredo Furelos

sponsored by LANIHAU CENTER

Gordon Lee received a BA from the University of Washington in 1964 and an MFA from University of Hawaii in 1972. He has taught ceramics at the Hawaii Community College since 1972. Gordon's most consistent theme is that of ceramic "Vessels," from whimsical to serious forms, from bottles to vases varying in character from traditional to original designs, from wheel thrown to hand built. He has a lost-wax cast bronze sculpture titled "Parade Rest" at the State

GORDON LEE

Capitol, a ceramic sculpture titled "International Utilitarian Device" at Kapiolani Hospital and was commissioned by the State Foundation on Culture and the Arts to complete recreational ceramic sculptures for the playground at Hilo Union School. The "BMX (Bike)" shown here is one of the items created to influence the thoughts of his students. Gordon explains, "Ceramics is not a media limited to 'usable' items. The BMX developed from the influence of my children, as have other non-functional ceramic items such as a trike, a family of ET's and a whimsical family of animals." Gordon's work can be seen at the Maya Gallery.

opposite right
BMX
ceramic
33 by 45 by 20 inches
collection of the artist
photograph by Linus Chao

sponsored by UNIVERSITY OF HAWAII - HILO

John Thomas is a versatile artist, a master of watercolor, oil and all drawing mediums. He is famous for watercolors of Hawaii's beautiful orchids and is equally famous for oil paintings of figures and tropical foliage, often incorporating Hawaiian legends. His newest oils are powerful constructions which appear to be geometric abstractions but actually are faithful to the biological shapes and growth patterns of their models in Nature. "The observer, looking closely at a portion of a banana leaf, sees perhaps a landscape. For the last few years I have been painting large oils in praise of Nature and inspired by the Gaea Theory. Nature is depicted as a self-contained force preoccupied with and motivated by grand schemes." John's work can be seen at Chocolate Orchid, Cunningham Gallery, Island Heritage Collection, Maya Gallery, Mauna Kea Beach Hotel, and Volcano Art Center.

JOHN THOMAS

opposite right
FIRE AND WATER
oil on linen
70 by 52 inches
collection of the artist
photograph by Alfredo Furelos
portrait photograph by Lee Thomas

sponsored by BRADLEY PROPERTIES, LTD.

The fiber wall constructions of Karron Nottingham Halverson demonstrate the artist's strong sense of design and composition and dramatic use of a palette of over one hundred colors. Design images range from abstract geometric compositions to organic forms emphasizing color relationships. This young artist has received numerous commissions and awards considerably beyond what one would expect for so short a professional career. Her fiber work is con-

KARRON
NOTTINGHAM HALVERSON

structed of 100% wool-wrapped manila hemp which makes these wall sculptures not only beautiful but durable as well. Her wall sculptures have been commissioned by the Japan Travel Bureau, Bank of Hawaii, Rumors Disco at the Ala Moana Hotel, Hawaii Insurance Company, First Bank Corporation (Wisconsin), Daiichi Corporation (Japan) and Mutual Insurance Company (Minnesota). She received the Jurors Award Best-of-Show at the Hawaii Craftsmen '88 show, Award for Excellence at the Hawaii Craftsmen '85 and two State Foundation on Culture and the Arts acquisition awards. Karron received a degree in Liberal Arts with Honors at the University of Wisconsin, River Falls and has studied at the Penland School of Crafts, Penland, North Carolina and the Haystack Hinckley School of Crafts, Hinckley, Maine. Karron is represented in Hawaii by the Fine Art Associates (Honolulu), Stones Gallery (Kauai) and in Los Angeles by the Del Mano Gallery. Her studio is Off The Wall on Furneaux Lane in downtown Hilo.

sponsored by HILO ACCIDENT & INDUSTRIAL
INJURY CLINIC

above
UNTITLED
fiber
8 by 6 feet
collection of Bank of Hawaii
photograph by Paul Kodama
portrait photograph by Christy Akiona

Jason Izumi was born and raised in Hawaii and began to paint full time on the Mainland in the mid 1980s. He enrolled at the prestigious Pratt Institute of Art and Design in Brooklyn and studied painting there for three years. In the summer of 1988 he studied in the Pratt-in-Venice, Italy fine arts program. He has also studied art history at Columbia University in New York City. Jason has exhibited his work in juried art shows and outdoor art festivals in Maine,

JASON IZUMI

New York, New Jersey, Pennsylvania, Connecticut and Hawaii where he has won numerous Best-In-Show and First Place awards. He has had several one man shows including in the Maine State Building, Poland Springs, Maine. A number of his pieces are in the collection of Mauna Lani Resort, Inc. In his painting "Mauna Lani I" Jason captures the silvery light sparkling off the waters. The reflections from the foliage on the bank cast mysterious shadows into the green depths of the lagoon near the Mauna Lani Bay Hotel bungalows. Jason's work is on permanent display at Teshima's Restaurant and Gallery in Honalo.

opposite right
MAUNA LANI I
acrylic
30 by 22 inches
collection of Mauna Lani Resort, Inc.
photograph by Alfredo Furelos

sponsored by MAUNA LANI RESORT, INC.

LINUS CHAO

Linus Chao was born in Shandong Province, China. His art and animation education started in Taiwan where he earned a BA degree in fine arts from the National Taiwan Normal University. Linus received several national art awards while in Taipei. In 1967 he was selected as one of ten "Outstanding Young Men" by the Jaycees of the Republic of China. Linus moved to Tokyo to study at the Toei Animation Studio and Gakkan Art Studio. He then moved to California to study cinematography at the University of Southern California. He received further training as an animation artist at the Walt Disney Production Studios. He also earned an MS degree from Parsons School of Design in New York. Linus has been an art instructor at the University of Hawaii at Hilo and Hawaii Community College since 1971. He is a versatile artist excelling in watercolor, brush painting, caligraphy, photography, cinematography and animation. His work has been displayed in Taiwan, Hong Kong, Brazil, El Salvador, Iran, Australia, Canada, Paris, New York, Los Angeles and San Francisco as well as in Hawaii. Linus has dedicated himself to building a bridge of understanding between the Chinese culture and that of his adopted country.

opposite right
HILO RAIN
watercolor
29 by 21 inches
collection of the artist
photograph by the artist

sponsored by UNIVERSITY OF HAWAII - HILO

When bowl turning is discussed in Hawaii Dan DeLuz's name is mentioned repeatedly because he partically single-handedly brought the craft into the latter half of the 20th century. Largely self taught, he has in turn taught most of the younger generation of Hawaii's bowl turners. The technique he has developed is masterful and results in bowls which will be cherished family heirlooms. Dan begins with the finest of native Hawaiian woods which he studies carefully

DAN DELUZ

in order to discover the most natural grain of the wood. Time is an important element in the curing of his bowls, often with a year passing between stages of their development. This results in the paper-thinness of his bowls which has made him justifiably famous. Painstaking care in sanding and finishing, "is what really makes the bowl," says Dan. "I strive for a silky smooth texture." The final stages are buffing, rubbing and then dipping in mineral oil to give the bowls a satin-like lustre. Koa is Dan's favorite wood, although he works in many different kinds of wood. His specialties are covered bowls and nested sets of bowls which are done with consummate mastery. Outstanding examples of Dan's work are on view at Hawaiian Handcraft in Hilo.

sponsored by MALAMA ARTS INC.

above
KOA WOOD BOWL
koa with *pewa* patches
8 by 13-3/4 inches
collection of the artist
photograph by Norman Makio

The Island of Hawaii has provided glass artist Wilfred Yamazawa with a rich source of poetic imagery which is translated into the visual arts through his glass sculpture. Each piece of Yamazawa Art Glass has been created solely by the artist as a unique work of art. The Yamazawa collection ranges from elegant, graceful and fragile pastels to a strong, sultry evocation of Hawaii's dramatic volcanoes. The islands' natural beauty is extolled in each of the

WILFRED YAMAZAWA

pieces, their names a reflection of nature's inspiration to his art. Wilfred was born in Honaunau, Kona, Hawaii and was raised on a coffee farm. He has received BFA and MFA degrees in sculpture at the University of Hawaii, Manoa. Wilfred has been widely shown in Hawaii through juried shows and exhibits at the Honolulu Academy of Arts, Hawaii Craftsman, Big Island Artists Guild and Volcano Arts Center. The Yamazawa Art Glass Studio is nestled in Holualoa village on the slopes of Mount Hualalai, Kona. His art glass is available at Volcano Art Center, Island Heritage Gallery in Waimea and at the Mark Masuoka Gallery in Las Vegas.

opposite right
PURPLE LILIES
blown glass
15 by 9 by 9, 12 by 9 by 9, 10 by 9 by 9 inches
collection of the artist
photograph by Alfredo Furelos

sponsored by THE HONOLULU ADVERTISER

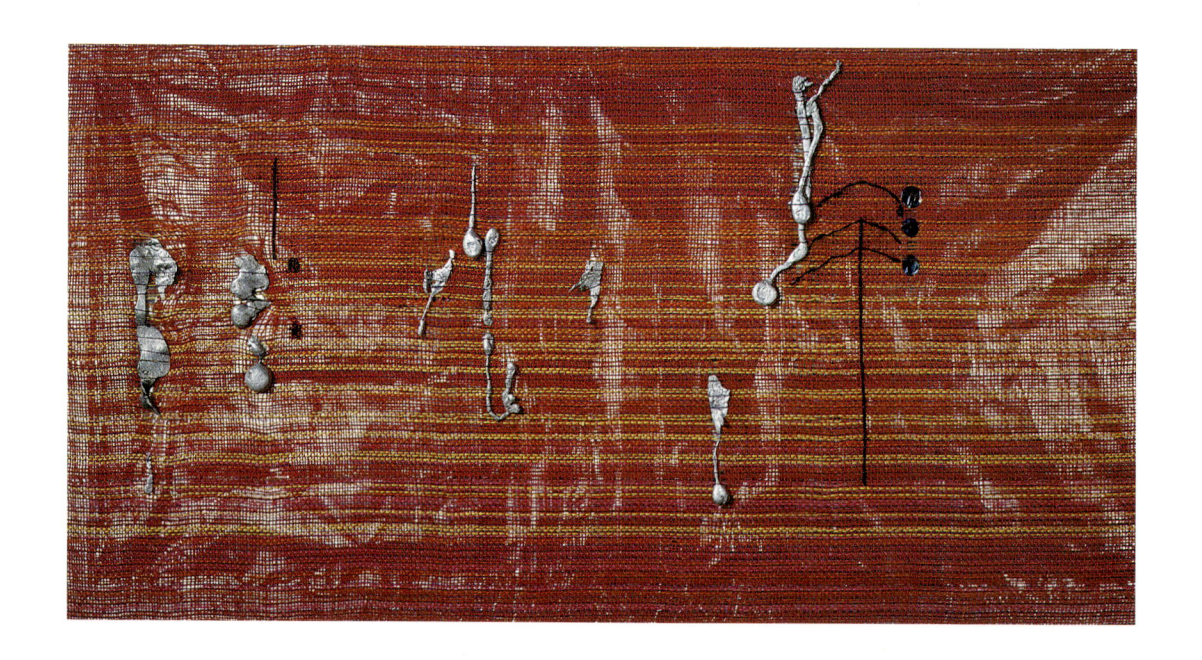

TERRIE RODMAN

JERRÉ TANNER

(above left and opposite right)
HOT! TO BLUES (DIPTYCH)
weaving with metal, both 22 by 40 inches
collection of the artist
photographs by Lee Thomas
(music: above, opposite right)
RED, BLUE
opening motives

Terrie Rodman has had a dynamic influence on the arts community of Hawaii Island in the few short years she has been living in Kona. Applying the knowledge she has gained from years of teaching creative development, Terrie has brought together artists and community leaders with the purpose of improving the Island's arts environment. She holds a MA degree in art and has had a successful career as an interior designer. While weaving and fiber arts have been her major focus, Terrie explores innovative techniques, such as sculpting Hawaii's gourds [see premiere edition page 36]. She merges into her weavings dyed metal segments, contrasting the textured surfaces of yarn and fibers with the smooth shimmering brilliance of these metals.

sponsored by PHYLLIS SELLENS & COMPANY

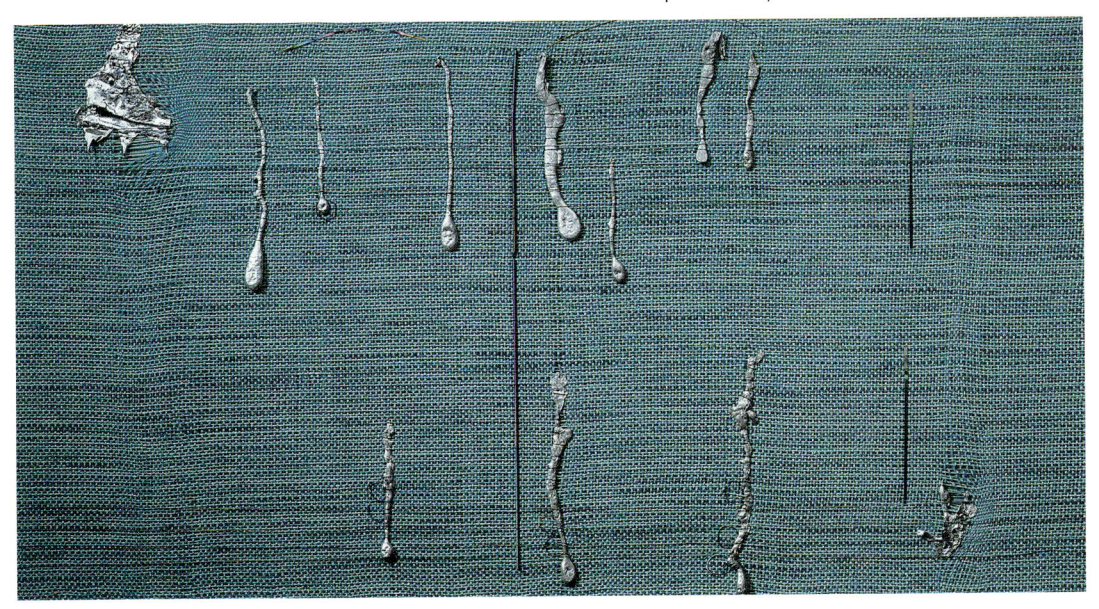

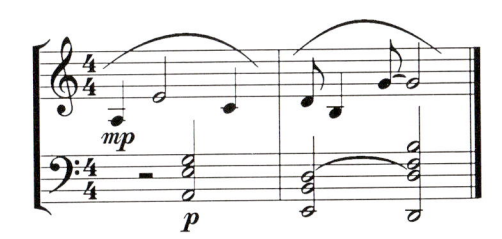

The original idea for *Hot! to Blues* emerged while Terrie was visiting an aluminum smelting plant. She watched hot liquid metal drop from thirty-foot vats to the ground, splattering into shapes that resembled musical notes and instruments. Terrie explained to me one cool afternoon at her mountain-side studio, "Without manipulating those metal images I went about dying linen, silks and niobium. Then I needed a composer to work with me in organizing those 'notes' into exciting original music, moving us from hot metal to cool product, hot music to cool rhythm." She, in turn, visited my studio in the sunny lowlands near the ocean. We worked at the computer and synthesizers until satisfied with the melodies and harmonies that were suggested by the dropped aluminum shapes.

sponsored by MULTI-ARTS INCORPORATED

LYNN ST AMAND

Lynn St.Amand's watercolor *Underwater Memories No. 9 "Pebbled Butterfly"* depicts one *lauhau*, pebbled butterfly (Chaetodon multicinctus), and two *lau-wiliwili-nukunuku-'oi'oi*, long nose butterfly (Lorcipiger flavissimus), and was painted from real life as observed at Kahalu'u Bay, Kona, Hawaii Island. Lynn says, "These innocent little fish will feed sometimes from my hand but are usually too shy." She was introduced to sea creatures as a child on her father's boat in Puget Sound. Lynn studied art at the Universitys of Washington and Alaska and has had 24 one man shows. In 1990 she participated in Malama Art's Invitational Exhibition at the Wailoa Center. Her work has appeared in *Honolulu* and *Spirit of Aloha, Alaska, Safari International* and on the cover of *the Northwest Journal of Canada*. Her watercolors of Hawaiian reef fish have been published by Multi-Arts as posters and fine arts note cards.

UNDERWATER MEMORIES NO. 9
watercolor, 24 by 30 inches
collection of Janice Stattin
photograph by Castleton, Anchorage, Alaska

sponsored ANONYMOUSLY

LAVA MASQUERADE
photography
16 by 20 inches
(continued on page 67)

BRAD LEWIS

sponsored by PERSONAL BUSINESS MANAGER

EDWIN MEDEIROS

POLYNESIAN CEREMONIAL DRUM
koa, cowhide, sisal
60 by 18 inches
collection of the artist
photograph by Alfredo Furelos
(continued on page 68)

sponsored by C. J. KIMBERLY REALTORS

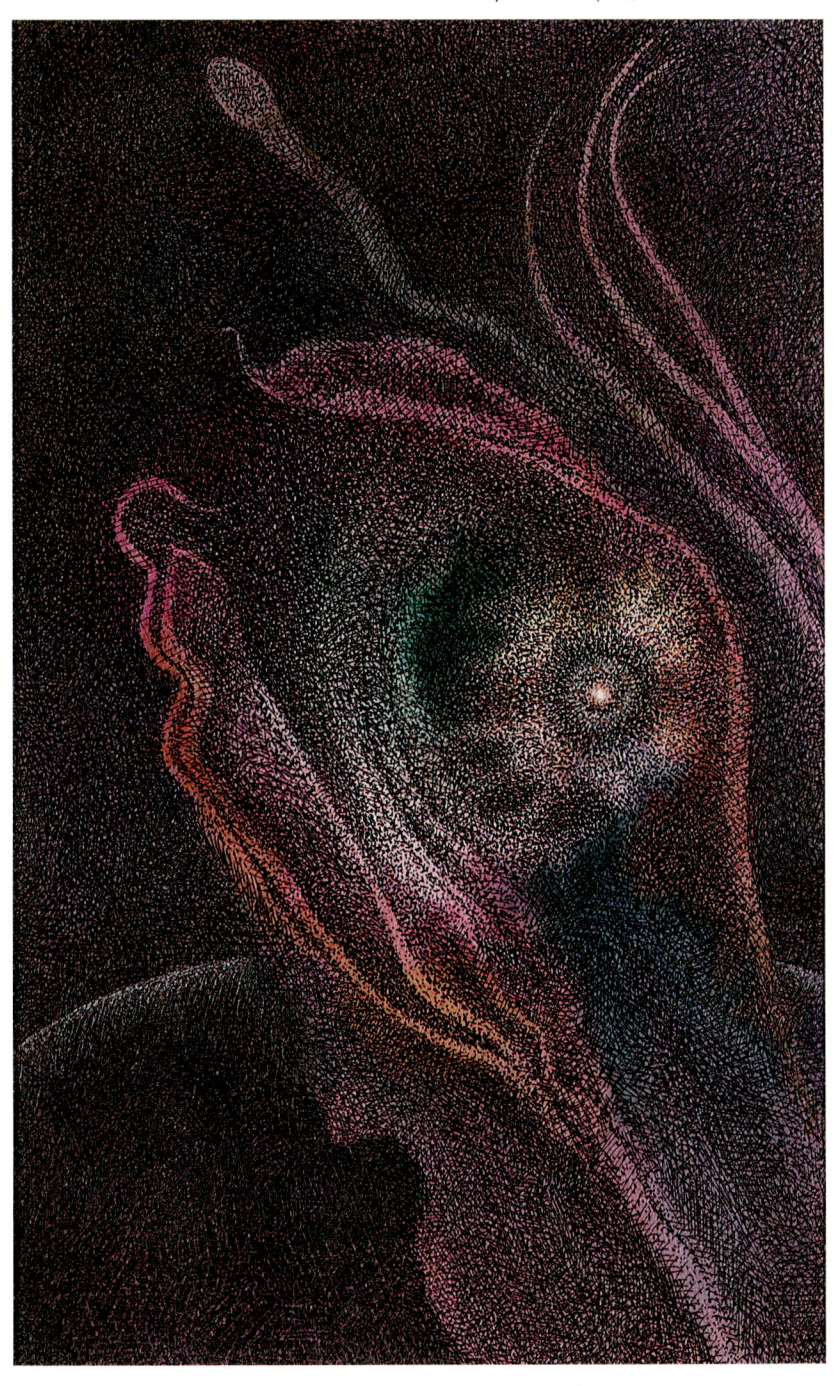

ANEMONE
pen and ink, ink washes, colored pencil
4-3/4 by 3 inches
photograph by The Lab, Tucson, Arizona
(continued on page 67)

DIANE McGREGOR

sponsored by LOYD'S ART SUPPLY

KENNETH LOYD

HAWAIIAN DREAM INTERIOR
oil, 40 by 30-3/8 inches
photograph by Norman Makio
(continued on page 67)

sponsored by WINKLER WOOD PRODUCTS, INC.

ANNE'S DESK
blonde ribbon curly koa, chocolate ribbon curly koa,
burgundy ribbon curly koa, blonde birdseye curly koa,
pheasant wood, sandalwood
38 by 32 by 18 (closed), 36 (open) inches
private collection
photograph by Alfredo Furelos
(continued on page 69)

GARY SOUKUP

DANIEL ANDERSON

sponsored by PUTMAN CLARK

MILES MASON

FISH IN THE BAMBOO
watercolor, 17 by 24-3/8 inches
photograph by Alfredo Furelos
(continued on page 67)

sponsored by KEAUHOU BEACH HOTEL

MILESTONES
photography, 7 by 5 inches
photograph developed at Alfredo's Photo Studio
(continued on page 69)

LEE PALAKIKO

sponsored by BLACKWELL CUSTOM WOODWORKS

PETER BLACKWELL

Peter Blackwell began a career in woodworking in the Florida Keyes. He spent five years rebuilding traditional wooden boats between Marathon and Key West. Arriving in *(continued on page 65)*

CHRISTMAS ROCKER
koa and velvet, 43 by 40 by 24 inches
collection of the artist
photograph by Alfredo Furelos

sponsored by FIBERARTS/TOPSTITCH

OCTOPUS GARDEN
silk painting, 48 by 36 inches
photograph by Alfredo Furelos
(continued on page 68)

JAN MOON

sponsored by ORCHID ISLE AUTO CENTER

RICHARD MORTEMORE

ON THE EDGE
acrylic, 30 by 22 inches
photograph by Alfredo Furelos
(continued on page 68)

sponsored by MICHAEL AND BETH KASSER

MARIAN BERGER-MAHONEY

Born in Ireland, Marian Berger-Mahoney spent early childhood on Wake Island and in Alaska. A resident of Hawaii since 1976 she has received numerous commissions. In 1987 she created a series of paintings of Kauai's most endangered birds and plants for the rooms at the Aston Kauai Resort. An edition of 2000 prints was published and proceeds from the sales were given to the Hawaii Nature Conservancy. Two of her pieces also appeared in the Bishop Museum 1988 American Association of *(continued on page 65)*

NUKUPU'U WITH KOKI'OKE'OKE'O BLOSSOMS
watercolor, 16 by 14 inches
collection of the artist
photograph by Modern Camera

sponsored by KONA RANCH HOUSE

JOANNE HENNES

HAWAIIAN FANTASY
oil, 60 by 30 inches
photograph by Fineprint Custom Photo Lab, Colorado
(continued on page 66)

sponsored by UPCOUNTRY QUILTERS

PUA MALE (STEPHANOTIS)
Hawaiian quilt
100 by 104 inches
collection of Mr. and Mrs. John C. Baldwin
photograph by J. Michael Kanouff
(continued on page 65)

SHARON BALAI

sponsored by MARYL DEVELOPMENT

VICKI SERVA

Vicki Serva is originally from Northern California and has lived in Kona for the past ten years. She is a member of the Hawaii Watercolor Society and has exhibited her paintings in numerous group shows on Hawaii Island and in Honolulu, including the Annual Spring Art Festival and "New Directions in Art" at Wailoa Center, Hilo. In 1990 she exhibited paintings in Malama Arts' Invitational Exhibition, also at Wailoa Center. Her watercolors and reproductions have been purchased for private collections as well as commercial developments in Hawaii, the Mainland, Canada, Europe, Japan, New Zealand and Australia. "Waterford" is part of a series of fractured pieces from The Crystal Collection of prints and note cards. Tropical Expressions is another of her series which is widely distributed. Her recent work can be seen at the Chocolate Orchid Gallery in Kona.

WATERFORD
watercolor, 22 by 30 inches
collection of John P. Dinmore
photograph by Alfredo Furelos

sponsored by HPM BUILDING SUPPLY

LONNY TOMONO

CHA-DANSU
koa and Okinawan linen (dyed by Barbara Tomono)
23 by 24 by 10-1/4 inches
private collection
photograph by Norman Makio
(continued on page 69)

sponsored by PEGGY CHESNUT & CO

TAI LAKE

HALL TABLE, A LINE STUDY
koa, black lacquer, 48 by 32 by 10 inches
collection of the artist
photograph by Alfredo Furelos
(continued on page 66)

sponsored by ALFREDO'S PHOTO STUDIO

ALFREDO FURELOS

Born and raised in Buenos Aires, Argentina, Alfredo began working in photography in 1970 as a Laboratory and Camera Assistant at Studio Manuel Bercovich. He attended the *Escuela Panamericana de Arte* in Buenos Aires studying photography for three years. From 1978 to 1985 Alfredo worked in his home city as a professional commercial photographer for Fiat, Renault, Chrysler, Ciba Geigy, Seiko, Bayer and more. Since moving to Hawaii Island in 1986 he has concentrated on photography for businesses with his work appearing in numerous publications including *The Waimea Gazette* and *Hawaii Island Artists and Friends of the Arts*. A particular specialty of his is photographing two and three dimensional fine art pieces. He recently had his Hawaii exhibition premiere in a one man show at the Kahilu Theatre. His business name is Alfredo's Photo Studio.

SUNSET BUBBLE
photograph
collection of the artist

sponsored by ART MART OF KONA

SUSAN PEZIM

NEW BEGINNINGS
acrylic/mixed media on canvas, 30 by 48 inches
(continued on page 69)

RANDY MOREHOUSE

TROPICAL FISH
raku ceramic, 7 by 14 inches each
(continued on page 68)

sponsored by HAWAII TRIBUNE HERALD

sponsored ANONYMOUSLY

LAU HALA MAT
lau hala (natural), 36 by 48 inches
(continued on page 66)

ELIZABETH LEE

SAMOAN TAPA, FLORAL TAPA, JUNGLE DRUMS
gouache on paper for reproduction on fabric
(continued on page 66)

BARBARA GARDNER

sponsored by REYN SPOONER INC.

sponsored by KEAUHOU-KONA REALTY, INC.

EDWIN KAYTON

SOUTH POINT
oil on canvas, 36 by 60 inches
(continued on page 66)

TEUNISSE BREESE-RABIN

RAKU PLATTER AND VASE TRIO
raku pottery, platter 13 by 13 by 3 inches, vases 16-3/4 by 25-1/4 by 34 inches *(continued on page 65)*

sponsored by KEAUHOU VILLAGE BOOK SHOP

sponsored by WAIMEA GENERAL STORE

A TRIO OF POTS
stoneware, platter 3 by 20 inches, sculpture 22 by 9
inches, bowl 4 by 12 inches *(continued on page 68)*

LEX MORRISS

KILAUEA'S MO'O
raku-fired clay, 30 inches long
(continued on page 65)

GARRON ALEXANDER

sponsored by FRIENDS OF GARRON ALEXANDER

sponsored by LISA CLARK

DIAN KNIGHT

ROSES -- A BAKER'S DOZEN
watercolor, 22-1/2 by 30 inches
(continued on page 66)

KEITH McGUIRE

PACIFIC GREEN
watercolor, pen and ink, 22 by 30 inches
(continued on page 68)

sponsored by AD STUDIO KONA

sponsored by MEADOW GOLD DAIRIES

HELICONIA CLEARING
fiber, painting and quilting, 45 by 60 inches
(continued on page 65)

FRED
oil, 18 by 24 inches
(continued on page 69)

CHRISTINE AHIA

HARRY WISHARD

sponsored by WILLIAM AND KATHLEEN JARDINE

63

sponsored by KAI MARKELL III

NALANI HUDDY MARKELL

'ALALA OF HUALALAI
watercolor and pencil, 22 by 30 inches
(continued on page 67)

SHELLY MAUDSLEY WHITE

SEA BUSINESS III
watercolor, 29-1/2 by 41-1/2 inches
(continued on page 67)

sponsored by ART MART OF KONA

FEATURED ARTISTS

(for Gallery key see page 114)

AHIA, CHRISTINE fiber
Sponsor: Meadow Gold Dairies
Collector: collection of the artist
Photographer: Alfredo Furelos
Galleries: Stones (Kauai), V A C
(continued from page 63) Christine's images are complemented with precision quilting along and beyond the contours of the paintings. Christine attended the University of Hawaii and received a BA in Art. Since 1970, her main focus has been textile design work. Many years of quilting, stitchery, and batik led to painting directly on the fabric. Christine says, "Many of my paintings are incorporated into functional items such as quilts and wearable art; I like to create pieces that are attractive, comfortable, and pleasing to wear and use."

ALEXANDER, GARRON crafts
Sponsor: The Friends of Garron Alexander
Collector: collection of the artist
Photographer: Alfredo Furelos
Galleries: Center, Gal Gt Things, Stones (Kauai), V A C
(continued from page 61) Garron received a BFA at Franklin and Marshall College in Lancaster, Pennsylvania and an MA at Reed College, Portland, Oregon. He began hand-building clay forms, firing them in wood-burning kilns. Moving to Hawaii in 1977, Garron has focused on clay sculpture. His sculpture has been acquired by The Honolulu Advertiser and included in numerous private collections. He has had commissions for bas-relief murals. He received recognition in the June, 1990 issue of *Studio Potter*, a national periodical.

BALAI, SHARON crafts
Sponsor: UpCountry Quilters
Galleries: Fiberarts
(continued from page 51) There are two aspects of creativity in Hawaiian quilt making -- the skill required to execute the stitching of a quilt and the design of the pattern to be quilted. Sharon Balai has specialized in creating unique and bold modern designs for this venerated old craft. After mastering the technical aspects of Hawaiian quilting Sharon branched off from traditional design patterns to create designs of her own which are at least as masterful as the traditional 19th. century designs which have been handed down to us. Sharon's outstanding ability to create these designs is quite rare.

BERGER-MAHONEY, MARIAN painting
Sponsor: Michael and Beth Kasser
Galleries: Bishop Mus (Oahu), Cunningham, Gal Gt Things, Haw Trop Bot Gn, Lyman, Showcase, Stones (Kauai), V A C
(continued from page 51) Museum Publications Competition. In 1988 she painted two watercolors presented to Senator Inouye and Representative Akaka for their contributions in preserving Hawaii's native wildlife. In June of 1988 she was commissioned to paint a mural for the Hyatt Regency Waikoloa.

BLACKWELL, PETER crafts
Sponsor: Blackwell Custom Woodworks
(continued from page 48) Hawaii in 1985 Peter found a need for custom woodworkers and spent the last five years working on custom homes in Hawaii. Peter has made display furniture for the Ellison Onizuka/NASA space museum at the Kona Airport. His ship working background inspired him to design furniture and architectural pieces with simple lines and smooth transitions. He builds functional pieces that are strong, durable and traditionally styled. Peter draws from design elements found in antique European and early American furniture and architectural pieces.

BREESE-RABIN, TEUNISSE crafts
Sponsor: Keauhou Village Book Shop
Collector: collection of the artist
Photographer: Diane McMillen
Galleries: Cottage Gal, V A C
(continued from page 60) Teunisse is equally skilled in functional stoneware, fine porcelain or raku. Her work is influenced by the contrasts of Hawaii Island. She is currently experimenting with different types of surfaces that emphasize the basic nature of the pot. A founding member of the Keauhou Potter's Guild, she located a communal studio suited to her preference to combine production with teaching. The studio is in the lower level of the SKEA building, a community cultural center she helped incorporate in 1981.

CHAO, LINUS painting
Sponsor: University of Hawaii at Hilo
(see pages 32-33)

DE LUZ, DAN crafts
Sponsor: Malama Arts Inc.
(see pages 34-35)

FURELOS, ALFREDO photography
Sponsor: Alfredo's Photo Studio
(see page 57)

GARDNER, BARBARA textiles
Sponsor: Reyn Spooner Inc.
Collector: designed exclusively for Reyn Spooner Inc.
Photographer: Rick Noyle
(continued from page 59) Barbara has studied at the California Polytechnic Institute as a Graphic Design major and at Hilo Community College in the Apparel Design Program. After her schooling she went directly into fabric design, although she continues to work with watercolor and oil. Barbara has designed fabrics for Reyn Spooner for three years.

GOMES, DAVID crafts
Sponsor: Mauna Lani Resort, Inc.
(see pages 18-19)

HENNES, JOANNE painting
Sponsor: Kona Ranch House Restaurant
Collector: Mr. and Mrs. Jacob Thomas
Galleries: MKBH Gallery, VAC
(continued from page 52) Joanne is a realist, finding her greatest inspiration in towering mountains, tropical jungles and rugged coastlines. Beginning her painting career in the Alps, she has traveled extensively from the deserts of Egypt to the jagged volcanic peaks of Hawaii and the wonders of New Zealand, capturing the varieties of nature on canvas. She has studied in Illinois, where she was born, and in Paris, France. Joanne finds the beauty of Hawaii to be a fresh and continuing challenge. Whether it be exotic tropical flowers or waterfalls in rain forests, she portrays in oils and watercolors. "Hawaiian Fantasy" has been published in a limited edition of lithographs.

IZUMI, JASON painting
Sponsor: Mauna Lani Resort, Inc.
(see pages 30-31)

KAIAMA, TSUGI crafts
Sponsor: Lanihau Center
(see pages 22-23)

KAYTON, EDWIN painting
Sponsor: Keauhou-Kona Realty, Inc.
Collector: collection of the artist
Photographer: artist
Agent: Art Source Hawaii Inc.
(continued from page 60) Ed Kayton's landscapes depict places, untouched by modern civilization, where man lived in harmony with his environment. In 1985 Kayton exhibited a sculpture series at the U.S Senate Rotunda sponsored by American Airlines. The series was then shown at the Hawaii State Capitol at the request of Governor John D. Waihee. Ed's life-size bronze bust of Col. Ellison Onizuka is in the NASA space museum at Kona Airport. Kayton's miniature sculpture of King Kalakaua was produced as a hologram on the cover of the centennial issue of *Honolulu* Magazine.

KNIGHT, DIAN painting
Sponsor: Lisa Clark
Collector: collection of the artist
Photographer: Alfredo Furelos
(continued from page 62) Dian Knight was inspired by an artistic mother who encouraged her talents. She earned a degree in Interior Design from Washington State University and directed a commercial design department in Portland, Oregon. After traveling and studying art Dian established her studio in Kona. She has recently returned from Japan where she studied Nihonga art, silk kimono painting, weaving and dyeing. She is a member of the Hawaii Watercolor Society, the West Hawaii Arts Guild and is a professional member of the American Society of Interior Designers.

LAKE, R. TAI crafts
Sponsor: Peggy Chesnut & Co.
Agent: Lake Construction
Galleries: Fiberarts, Maya
(continued from page 56) Son of a master craftsman, Tai gained an early familiarity with a wide variety of tools and materials. He studied studio art/graphic design at Southern Illinois University. Since moving to Hawaii commissioned work and construction projects has kept his free time at a premium. "I sense that it is time for me to switch from carrying a running backlog to creating a 'prolog,' creating pieces that need to be seen. Boundaries have to be explored in order to expand appreciation for craft and craft-as-art at this point in history." Tai lives in Holualoa and continues to seek the proper combination of skill, materials, and refinement of line.

LEE, ELIZABETH MALU'IHI AKO crafts
Sponsor: anonymous
Collector: Reginald and Donna Lee
Photographer: Ed Gross
(continued from page 59) Elizabeth Lee is recognized as one of the most outstanding *lau hala* weavers in Hawaii. She began weaving as a child under the supervision of her *hanai* mother Hattie Kahananui, later with her mother Lilly Ako. As an adult she studied with Mrs. Kimura. The mat depicted here shows Elizabeth's total control of her medium. The semi-circular movements radiating out from the center adds a shimmering brilliance to the work. The *lau hala* is its

natural color, it is not bleached. The types of weave used are *piko maka pawehe, pawehe loa* and *pawehe palua.*

LEE, GORDON crafts
Sponsor: University of Hawaii at Hilo
(see pages 24-25)

LEWIS, G BRAD photography
Sponsor: anonymous
Galleries: Chocolate Orchid, Gal Gt Things, Pahoa, VAC
(continued from page 41) Brad Lewis is a quiet, gentle man with a strong commitment to preserving the environment of our beautiful planet. He started photographing the scenic wonders of Utah as a child and began traveling world-wide in his teens. After attending the University of Utah he moved to Alaska where he distinguished himself in diverse ways including being a Field Investigator for the Bureau of Indian Affairs and completing a geologic map of the Arrigetch Peaks, Brooks Range. He established his home in Hawaii in 1984 and continued traveling extensively throughout the Pacific Basin. His spectacular color photographs of volcanic activity have brought his work to international attention. His photographs have appeared in *Time, Life, Omni, Sierra, the New York Times, Geo, Aloha* and other periodicals.

LOYD, KENNETH painting
Sponsor: Loyd's Art Supply
Collector: W. C. Loyd
Galleries: Loyd's Art Supply
(continued from page 44) Kenneth Loyd has been painting on Hawaii Island for the past five years. He and his wife are the founders of Loyd's Art Supply, a major source for artist materials on the Island. Ken attended the Dallas Art Institute and studied privately with master oil painter Maggie McGill. He also studied serigraphy (silk screen) with Charles Phillips. Kenneth has been selling to private collectors for twenty years. His work ranges from abstracts to objective surrealism.

MARKELL, NALANI HUDDY painting
Sponsor: Kai Markell III
Collector: collection of the artist
Photographer: Alfredo Furelos
Galleries: V A C
(continued from page 64) Nalani is island-born, a Kamehameha Schools and University of Hawaii graduate. Her career began in 1987 as artist-assistant to actor/artist Tony Curtis. In 1989 she was chosen by Governor Waihe'e for the first Japanese-sponsored "Ship for World Youth" program and was honored by the State in 1989 with a Certificate on the Senate floor for "her expression of the Aloha tradition." Of Hawaiian, Chinese, Irish, French and Seneca heritage, she feels each has contributed to her love of nature.

MASON, MILES painting
Sponsor: Putman Clark
Collector: collection of the artist
Galleries: Choc Orch, Cunningham, V A C
(continued from page 46) Miles Mason's work is "an expression of the visual and emotional impact the tropics have made upon my life." His adult life, work, and travels have been spent in seeking tropical vision. After graduation from the University of California, with a degree in anthropology, Miles has lived and worked in Tonga, Iraq, Trinidad, Aruba and Indonesia. A long-held dream of living and working in Hawaii eventually brought Miles to the Islands in 1987. Miles's red-green color blindness has led him to develop innovative and non-traditional uses of the watercolor medium, resulting in an intensity of color unusual to the medium.

MAUDSLEY WHITE, SHELLY painting
Sponsor: Art Mart of Kona
Collector: Susan Pezim
Photographer: Ed Gross
Galleries: Art Mart, Isl Heritage
(continued from page 64) Born and raised in California, Shelly moved to Hawaii and attended the Honolulu Artisan School of Interior Design. Her work has been selected as the decor for the Waikoloa Beach Club adjacent to the Hyatt Regency at Waikoloa. Shelly likes to work on a large scale and has recently been commissioned to complete a 4 by 14 foot lagoon piece for the Holua Restaurant at Mauna Loa Village. Several of her images have been chosen to be part of the Island Heritage Collection.

MCGREGOR, DIANE graphics
Sponsor: C. J. Kimberly Realtors
Collector: collection of the artist
(continued from page 43) Diane received a BFA at the University of Arizona in Tucson in 1985. She received a graduate internship at the University Museum, assisting in research and cataloging their print collection. In Moscow in 1986 Diane attended the encounter of the Soviet Vega spacecraft with Halley's Comet. Her pen and ink illustrations of the comet's nucleus have been published in *Nature* and *Sky and Telescope.* In 1988 she participated in *New Directions in Art*, a juried show at the Wailoa Center. She was included in *Drawing 1989*, a national competition sponsored by Brigham Young University and curated by Thomas Padon of the Guggenheim Museum. Recently, her work was included in *American Drawing Biennial* at the College of William and Mary in Williamsburg, Virginia.

MCGUIRE, R. KEITH painting
Sponsor: Ad Studio Kona
Collector: Lionel Kutner
Photographer: Ad Studio Kona
Galleries: Choc Orch, Collectors Galleries (Sarasota and Venice, Florida)
(continued from page 62) Keith's subjects for his detailed watercolors come from his interest in wildlife and botanical studies. Largely self-taught, Keith has developed his own watercolor style. At the Center for Creative Studies in Detroit he discovered a preference for illustration which he combined with his love of animals. On Hawaii Island Keith has created many works featuring indigenous and endangered species, such as the *nene* goose and the sea turtle.

MEDEIROS, EDWIN crafts
Sponsor: Personal Business Manager
Galleries: VAC
(continued from page 42) This *pahu* has been carved from a 700 lb. log found in the *mauka* Kaloko area of Hawaii Island. The female spirit of the tree inspired Ed to form the drum as a tribute to the culture of the ancient Hawaiian people. The base is a carving of six *menehune* acrobats on their hands holding up the drum. It is lashed in an intricate Polynesian pattern using sisal. Ed is a native of Hawaii Island. Over the past twenty years he has created many sculptures of koa, milo and basalt stone. His sculptures are depictions of Hawaiian mythology as well as endemic Hawaiian bird and animal images. Ed also enjoys integrating Polynesian form with modern concepts in the medium of polychrome and assemblage. His work is exhibited in numerous art centers in Hawaii and on the Mainland.

MOON, JAN fiber
Sponsor: Fiberarts/Topstitch
Collector: Fiberarts
Galleries: Fiberarts
(continued from page 49) An artist and naturalist, Jan Moon paints lifelike renderings of birds, fish, plants, insects and mythical creatures. She uses French dyes on 100% China silk. "Silk is very mysterious and has a life of its own, as does nature. They both must be treated with respect and must be left free." Her work is strongly influenced by oriental art, methods and traditions. Jan has traveled extensively around the world living in remote villages learning from the people their individual arts and culture. A long time resident of Hawaii she is inspired by the multicultural mix of its people and the extraordinary beauty of its environment. Jan has exhibited in galleries in Hawaii and Japan.

MOREHOUSE, RANDY crafts
Sponsor: Hawaii Tribune Herald
Collector: collection of the artist
Photographer: Alfredo Furelos
Galleries: Gallery of Great Things, Showcase Gallery, Chocolate Orchid, Volcano Art Center, Stones Gallery (Kauai), Following Sea (Oahu)
(continued from page 58) These ceramic fish were thrown on a potter's wheel and then manipulated by hand. They have been glazed with copper mat and raku fired. Randy Morehouse studied ceramics at the University of Puget Sound. After graduation in 1974 he came to Hawaii where he has been making functional stoneware and porcelain. "I find clay to be the most wonderful of media. It begins as a soft lump receptive to any shape one can imagine. Then, once surrendered to the fire, it becomes a rigid, strong and permanent material."

MORRISS, LEX crafts
Sponsor: Waimea General Store
Title: "A Trio of Pots"
Collector: collection of the artist
Photographer: Alfredo Furelos
Galleries: Waimea General Store
(continued from page 61) Lex Morriss is a self-taught potter. He was raised on Maui and Hawaii Island. Lex has made pottery for 15 years and is currently working out of a studio at his home. His work is available exclusively at the Waimea General Store. While accepting an occasional commission, Lex prefers to work on his own. He has received A State Foundation for Culture and the Arts Purchase Award.

MORTEMORE, RICHARD painting
Sponsor: Orchid Isle Auto Center
Collector: collection of the artists
Galleries: Showcase, VAC, Pacific Island Art (Oahu)
(continued from page 50) Richard Mortemore has been painting wildlife for over twenty years. His abiding interest in the environment has prompted him to publish a series of nature guides on Hawaiian Wildlife (written with his wife Judith), write articles on wildlife for national publications, and become the director the the Keakealani Outdoor Education Center at Volcano. He has received the State of Hawaii Conservation Award for his work in environmental education for the children of Hawaii. The care he takes to place birds and animals in their natural habitat has brought his work to the attention of periodicals such as *Wildlife Art News*. His paintings are in private collections in 14 states.

NOTTINGHAM HALVERSON, KARRON fiber
Sponsor: Hilo Accident & Industrial Injury Clinic
(see pages 28-29)

PALAKIKO, LEE photography
Sponsor: Keauhou Beach Hotel
(continued from page 47) "Milestones" is the second in a trilogy "The Cosmic Stone-Age," a trilogy of abstract images playing on the concepts of time and values. Today, we are all aware of the past, present and future. Being of Hawaiian ancestry, the conflict of time is very significant. The past represents *na kupuna*, our ancestors who established our values. Then *na makua*, our parents who reinforced those values; and lastly, *na kamaiki*, our children of the future that will implement these values with confidence and creativity. Thus, cornerstones, stepping stones and milestones, expresses the very principle of universal peace and harmony through the power of the aloha spirit; the ultimate goal of mankind.

PEZIM, SUSAN HANSON painting
Sponsor: Art Mart of Kona
Photographer: Ed Gross
(continued from page 58) Born in Newport South Wales, Great Britain, Susan has painted in oils since she was 13. In 1988 she discovered acrylics and studied under Pamela Holl Hunt in Canada. She moved to Kona in early 1989 and has studied under many of the Island's best local artists. Susan also owns Art Mart of Kona which has provided her with constant contact with the local art community.

RODMAN, TERRIE crafts
Sponsor: Phyllis Sellens & Company
Galleries: Volcano Art Center
(see pages 38-39)

SALMOIRAGHI, FRANCO photography
Sponsor: The Honolulu Advertiser
(see pages 20-21)

SERVA, VICKI painting
Sponsor: Maryl Development
(see page 54)

SEXTON, LLOYD painting
Sponsor: Mauna Kea Beach Hotel
(see pages 14-17)

SOUKUP, GARY/ANDERSON, DAVID crafts
Sponsor: Winkler Wood Products Inc.
(continued from page 45) Fine craftsmanship and careful selection of materials, combined with years of experience working together, result in pieces both functional and artistic. "Each piece is crafted to the client's personal needs and specifications," explains David Anderson. In 1973 Gary Soukup began design and construction of fine furniture pieces in wood and leather. Since moving to Hawaii in 1975 he has continued this work with a focus on blending the fine local woods into art furniture. In 1970 David Anderson apprenticed as a boat builder for two years and continued boat construction in the Pacific Northwest until moving to Hawaii in 1980. David and Gary met in 1982. Their common interest in woodwork has developed into a working relationship which is both dynamic and harmonious.

ST AMAND, LYNN painting
Sponsor: Multi-Arts Incorporated
(see page 40)

THOMAS, JOHN painting
Sponsor: Bradley Properties, Ltd.
(see pages 26-27 and page 85)

TOMONO, LONNY MASARU crafts
Sponsor: HPM BUilding Supply
Galleries: Maya, VAC, Gallery EAS (Oahu), Stones (Kauai)
(continued from page 55) Born in Hilo, Lonny Tomono has studied at the University of Hawaii at Hilo, San Francisco Art Institute and San Jose State University. While in the Bay Area Lonny apprenticed with Makoto Imai, a master Kyoto Temple Builder. He then apprenticed for six years with Seiichiro Kitamura in Kyoto, Japan. In 1987 he returned to Hawaii Island with his wife Barbara, an accomplished textiles artist, and established Volcano Studio. He began showing his work in group shows, including the Hawaii Craftsmen Annual Shows, and a one man show at Gallery EAS, Honolulu. His sculpture combines traditional Japanese woodworking technique with a modern eye for materials and abstraction. His furniture pieces in wood, stone and other materials are earning for Lonny a much deserved reputation for achievement.

WISHARD, HARRY painting
Sponsor: William and Kathleen Jardine
Collector: William and Kathleen Jardine
Photographer: Alfredo Furelos
Galleries: Gallery of Great Things, VAC
(continued from page 63) Known for his landscapes, Harry Wishard also paints portraits in a highly individualistic style intended to bring out the personality of the subject. Living in Waimea with his wife and children, views of the Waimea hills and upcountry vistas are major subjects for his painting. He began painting and drawing at an early age in the plantation town of Pahala. He has been exhibiting his work in Honolulu and on Hawaii Island since 1982. Harry is the nephew of painter Lloyd Sexton [see pages 14 to 17].

YAMAZAWA, WILFRED crafts
Sponsor: The Honolulu Advertiser
(see pages 36-37)

ARTIST
BENEFACTORS

UNIVERSITY OF HAWAII AT HILO

With an enrollment 0f 4,000, UHH is part of Hawaii's nine campus system of higher education, currently incorporating a College of Arts and Sciences with the Hawaii Community College, a College of Agriculture, and a Center for Continuing Education and Community Service. In 1987 UHH-WEST HAWAII was established as an Outreach Higher Education Center. To develop human potential to the fullest extent possible through an intellectually stimulating environment is the educational philosophy of UHH. Students may select from a variety of vocational and academic options: 24 certificate/associate degrees and 24 baccalaureate degrees in arts, agriculture, business administration and computer science.

Hilo, Hawaii • 96720-4091 • 933-3311

LANIHAU CENTER

DISCOVER "ALOHA" AT LANIHAU! West Hawaii's shopping center, conveniently located in the heart of Kailua-Kona. Enjoy over twenty specialty shops, restaurants and services with unlimited free and easy parking in a beautiful turn of the century Hawaii shopping environment.

75-5595 Palani Road • Kailua-Kona, Hawaii 96740 • 329-9333

HILO ACCIDENT & INDUSTRIAL INJURY CLINIC

"Health Through Chiropractic" • Dr. Kurt Halverson, D.C.
PAIN treatment by the friendly professionals of Hilo's most complete facility • serving the Hilo community for 8 years
24 hour emergency service • located at Waiakea Office Plaza

345 Kekuanaoa Street, Suite 32 • Hilo, Hawaii 96720 • 961-6373

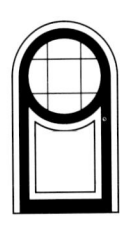

BLACKWELL CUSTOM WOODWORKS

custom doors • windows
furniture • specialty items
using native and imported
hardwoods
to your specifications

74-5583 Pawai Place • Kailua-Kona
Hawaii 96740 • 326-3221

FIBERARTS / TOPSTITCH

specializes in Hawaiian quilts, wallhangings and beautiful Hawaiian print fabrics. Our one-of-a-kind wearable ART clothing, created by local artists, are treasures in any wardrobe. Also available are patterns, kits and items for the Fiberarts crafter.
Parker Ranch Shopping Center
P O Box 2631 • Kamuela, Hawaii
96743 • 885-7666

BRADLEY PROPERTIES LTD

is known for quality real estate services and premiere properties. Three locations: WAIMEA 885-6077; WAIKOLOA 883-9606; KONA 329-5255

75-5722 Kuakini Hwy • Rm 103 • Kailua-Kona, Hawaii 96740

THE PERSONAL BUSINESS MANAGER

provides business and personal
income tax preparation and
consulting,
accounting and payroll services,
and computer consulting
with a special sensitivity to the needs
of artists and collectors of fine art.
75-5722 Kuakini Hwy •Suite 104C
Kailua-Kona, Hawaii 96745
329-4811

Meadow Gold
HAWAII'S DAIRY

"the Company that
cares about the
Big Island"

Hilo • 935-5482
Kona • 322-3900

ART MART

Largest selection of
fine artists' supplies
on the Big Island

complete matting and framing
services

Palm Terrace • 74-5615 Luhia St.
Kailua-Kona, Hawaii 96740
326-1301

---

garron alexander

GARRON ALEXANDER CERAMICS STUDIO
ceramic imagery ranging from
Hawaiian mythology (see page 61)
through marine-life and flowers, and
from tile murals to jewelry
Commissions are accepted.
P O Box 501 • Volcano, Hawaii
96785 • 967-7677
sponsored by
Friends of Garron Alexander

KEAUHOU-KONA REALTY, INC.

is a full service brokerage serving all of your Real Estate needs. We are conveniently located in the Keauhou Shopping Village. Visit one of our friendly professionals at our Keauhou Shopping Village office at

78-6831 Alii Drive Ste 109 • Kailua-Kona, Hawaii 96740 • 322-3101

MALAMA ARTS INC.

a source of information on
the arts of Hawaii Island
crafts
artists
galleries
art centers
recent print publications

P O Box 1478 • Kailua-Kona
Hawaii 96745 • 329-5828

Keauhou Beach HOTEL *Kona, Hawaii*

Salutes the local artists and their
vision to express creative viewpoints
through the cultural dimensions of
Hawaii

78-6740 Alii Drive
Kailua-Kona, Hawaii 96740
322-3441

PEGGY CHESNUT & CO.
Interior Design
74-5616 Luhia Street • Kailua-Kona, Hawaii 96740 • 329-8272

UpCountry Quilters

UPCOUNTRY QUILTERS

specializes in Hawaiian Quilt patterns and Hawaiian Pillow and Wall Hanging Kits. They are available in fine gift and craft shops throughout Hawaii. Designs are by Sharon Balai.

P O Box 2631 • Kamuela, Hawaii 96743 • 885-7666

MAUNA KEA BEACH HOTEL

From 30 precious Hawaiian quilts, commissioned by Laurance S. Rockefeller over 25 years ago, and lithographed floral prints by the late beloved Hilo-born Lloyd Sexton, to a new full-color book, The Art of Mauna Kea, authored by Big Island resident Dr. Don Aanavi with photography by David Franzen, the Mauna Kea continues its tradition of commitment to Hawaii's arts.

One Mauna Kea Beach Drive • Kohala Coast, Hawaii 96743-9706
882-7222

C. J. KIMBERLY REALTORS

Specializing in oceanfront, commercial and quality residential properties. Now located in the Kimberly Realty Center on Kahakai Road next to the Kona Hilton.

P O Box 5600 • Kailua-Kona, Hawaii 96745 • 329-9363

MAUNA LANI RESORT

salutes those Hawaii Island artists whose creative vision adds an essential dimension to our Island home, those artists with the determination to grow professionally though isolated and far from the mainstream of art.

It is Mauna Lani's policy to draw upon Island art resources whenever possible. In order to encourage Hawaii Island talent, Mauna Lani Resort lends its support to the art community in the form of an annual art competition with substantial cash prizes.

P O Box 4959 • Kohala Coast, Hawaii 96743-4959 • 885-6677

Hawaii TRIBUNE-HERALD

Supports Hawaii Island Artists

355 Kinoole Street • Hilo, Hawaii 96720 • 935-6621

1030 Kanoelehua Avenue
Hilo, Hawaii 96720
935-1191

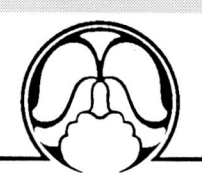

75-5633 Palani Road
Kailua-Kona, Hawaii 96740
329-4851

Orchid Isle Auto Center
FORD • LINCOLN • MERCURY • ISUZU • LAFORZA • DAIHATSU

HPM BUILDING SUPPLY

color
your world
with the best
Benjamin Moore Paints

Benjamin Moore PAINTS

Hilo	Waimea	Kona
935-0875	885-6036	329-1634

MARYL DEVELOPMENT, INC.

is pleased and very proud to help support our local Island artists. Their art is represented in the design and decor of our homes and will continue to be featured in all of our future developments.

P O Box 1928 • Kailua-Kona
Hawaii 96745 • 329-0866

HOLUALOA MANAGEMENT CORPORATION

I. MICHAEL KASSER
President

P O Box 323 • Holualoa, Hawaii
96725 • 322-2155 • FAX 322-0029

Loyd's Art Supply

LOYD'S ART SUPPLY

• Best Selection
• Best Prices
• Best Service
owned & operated by artists

262 Kamehameha Ave
Hilo, Hawaii 96720
961-ARTS

MULTI-ARTS INCORPORATED

produces the HAWAIIAN CLASSICAL MUSIC SERIES recordings featuring Jerré Tanner, Hawaii's leading symphonic and operatic composer, and publishes the HAWAII CONTEMPORARY SERIES fine arts note cards and offset lithographs, currently featuring Lynn St. Amand and Phan Nguyen Barker.

P O Box 1478 • Kailua-Kona, Hawaii 96745 • 329-5828

THE CONTEMPORARY MUSEUM

exhibiting, interpreting, collecting and preserving art of the last four decades
2411 Makiki Heights Drive • Honolulu, Hawaii 96822 • 526-1322
sponsored by The Honolulu Advertiser

The Honolulu Advertiser
Covering Hawaii since 1856

supports the arts and Hawaii's contemporary artists

605 Kapiolani Boulevard • Honolulu, Hawaii 96813

ALFREDO FURELOS, PHOTOGRAPHER

commercial • advertising
architectural • interior decoration
food and packaging • portraits
color, b/w, transparencies,
cibachrome
large format camera our specialty

P O Box 2281 • Kamuela, Hawaii 96743 • 885-4362

WINKLER WOOD PRODUCTS INC.
is proud to serve Hawaii in three locations - Hilo, Kona, and Honolulu, as the leading producer of fine Hawaiian Koa lumber. We offer the widest selection of local and exotic hardwoods, flooring, and special milling catering to your needs. Come and see our showroom.
**261-A Kekuanaoa Street
Hilo, Hawaii 96720 • 961-6411**

Reyn's

Long recognized as Hawaii's leader in traditional sportswear and classic clothing for men and women, our reputation is based on our uncompromising attention to quality, detail and service. As a Reyn's customer, you are always our most important consideration.

Locations: Kamuela, Lahaina, Kapalua, Honolulu and Waipoli

KEAUHOU VILLAGE BOOK SHOP

is pleased to support the Artists of Hawaii and to offer a selection of books, prints, stationery, audio and video cassettes and gift items which feature their work. Located in the Keauhou Shopping Village.

78-6831 Alii Drive, Ste 135 • Kailua-Kona, Hawaii 96740 • 322-8111

Kona Ranch House

Delicious food and friendly service in a casual turn-of-the-century Hawaiiana atmosphere; up-country, homestyle cookin' at family prices in two comfortable dining rooms; breakfast, lunch and dinner from 6:30 am; dinner reservations recommended for the Plantation Lanai Room

Kuakini Hwy above the Shell station
75-5653 Ololi Street • Kailua-Kona Hawaii 96740 • 329-7061

ASK Ad Studio Kona

Full service advertising agency provides campaign and media planning, with creative design and production in all media. Consultancy service for small clients and community groups. Company image packages include logo, brochure, advertisements.

329-1901
P O Box 3210
Kailua-Kona, Hawaii 96745

WAIMEA GENERAL STORE

Waimea's original country store. We offer Peter Hayward originals, pottery by Lex Morriss, needlepoint canvases, yarn and more. When you think kitchen accessories or gifts, remember us.
located in Parker Square

P O Box 187 • Kamuela, Hawaii 96743 • 885-4479

PHYLLIS SELLENS & COMPANY

When it comes to the "Art of Living" we at Phyllis Sellens & Company will be pleased to assist you in finding just the right home or real estate investment to compliment your collection.
Robert L. Bates (R), Phyllis Sellens & Co.
Real Estate Opportunities 329-7726, 325-7103 FAX 329-5798

77-6425 Kuakini Hwy Ste 101 • Kailua-Kona, Hawaii 96740

REBECCA CROCKETT moved to Kona just two years ago after nearly a decade and a half of distinguished accomplishments in Honolulu. She has been active in Public Relations with several well known Island firms, among them Patti Cook & Associates. She has been Director of Public Relations at the Royal Waikoloan and Marketing Programs Coordinator for Aston Hotels and Resorts. Her work for Aston resulted in her writing and producing a series of historical brochures featuring sites on the four major Hawaiian Islands. These brochures, written for both visitors and residents alike, emphasized the cultural and historical importance of these sites with preservation being the ultimate message. Rebecca is an avid student of Hawaiian culture and has contributed to it in various projects. She was Research Editor for *The Hula*, the definitive book on Hawaii's greatest cultural achievement. She also contributed numerous articles for magazines and newsletters including *Press Woman* (the National Federation of Press Women magazine), *Kahala 5000* (The Kahala Hilton Newsletter) and *The Punahou Bulletin* (Punahou School's Alumni magazine).

HENRY WEEKS
1836 - 1912

HENRY WEEKS
KONA'S MASTER
WOODWORKER

In the early 1800's the town of Hilo, Hawaii was the bustling center of population, trade and commerce on the Big Island of Hawaii. Henry Weeks, Sr. arrived, as many just like him in those early days of the Hawaiian Kingdom, full of hopes and dreams. He was also looking for a Hawaiian wife. However, he brought with him something no one else could boast at the time -- the skills of an English cabinetmaker, the first to settle in the Kingdom.

He soon became a naturalized citizen of the Kingdom, and it is recorded that he was granted a parcel of land by His Majesty King Kamehameha III in 1834. He later married a Hawaiian woman, Keka'aloa, who presented him with a handsome son in 1836, Henry Weeks, Jr.

Under the expert tutelage of his father, young Henry learned the skills of a craftsman, using the native hardwoods of Hawaii to produce fine furniture and other items.

Henry was eager to put his apprenticeship to work and in 1859, at the age of twenty-three, he boldly set out on his own. He moved the distant 135 miles from Hilo to the remote district of Kona. In those times it took several days by horse trail to reach the west shore of the Big Island, so it must have been a sad day for his mother. Young Henry, being cut from the same cloth as his adventurous father, probably saw the move as a marvelous adventure.

For his place of residence, he chose the cool upper regions of North Kona and settled just off the rocky horse trail in the sleepy village of Kainaliu in the region known as *Kalukalu*. He supported himself by doing woodwork and construction for the residents of the Kona and Ka'u districts, and in 1860 he married another part-Hawaiian, Rebecca Hall, the daughter of an Englishman.

He established himself in the district as a general blacksmith, shodding the horses of residents as well as those of passing travelers. He advertised himself as a carpenter, woodturner, cooper, wheelwright and canoe maker. He touted his expertise in the

STATISTICAL AND COMMERCIAL DIRECTORY & TOURIST GUIDE for 1880 boasting, "... only the very best of workmen and use of the best materials..."

Indeed, he had by this time gained quite a reputation as a master woodworker. It is recorded that he did extensive work at Huli-he'e Palace building chairs, installing moulding and fashioning a beautiful sofa which is still housed in the Palace. It is also worth noting that all wood work in this period was done strictly by hand. There were no power tools. Each piece was wrought after long and patient study with little tolerance for trial and error.

The fine line between 'craftsman' and 'artisan' was clearly evident when a person of Henry Weeks' ability took in hand a piece of wood, visualizing what was contained within, even before he began to work it. And then, miraculously, it seemed that all he had to do was remove the excess wood from the final piece that had always existed within the raw timber. Every now and then, an exceptional piece of wood came into the hands of an exceptional artisan which produced extraordinary results. Such was the work of Henry Weeks.

Hawaiian woodworkers were noted for their knowledge of the workability and peculiarities of different native woods. Any artisan working with Hawaiian wood had to know the qualities of the particular wood -- not just its obvious beauty or ability to take a high polish. For example, many people made *koa* the wood of choice because it was plentiful, beautiful and was a widely accepted native hardwood. But artisans such as Henry Weeks must have also been acquainted with the beauty and quality of lesser known yet far more valuable woods such as *kauila* and *uhiuhi*, just to mention a few.

Koa forests were plentiful during this period. Rancher Henry Greenwell notes in a June, 1874 journal entry that Henry Weeks paid the Minister of the Interior the sum of only ten dollars for the privilege of cutting *koa* trees for one year. Greenwell also notes that Weeks made regular repairs to his wagons, hauled wood to the beach for shipment and built household furniture. Greenwell descendants still use a *koa* four-poster bed crafted by Weeks some time between 1875 and 1880. Weeks took furniture orders from Kona residents and made each piece painstakingly by hand.

There are also many references to the fact that Mr. Weeks made other contributions to the community such as making improvements to the ship landings at Kainaliu and Napo'opo'o as well as fashioning canoes there. It must have been these things that caught the eye of young Prince Jonah Kuhi'o who was fond of vacationing at Napo'opo'o, for in 1902 he commissioned Weeks to build "the fastest racing canoe in the Islands."

The famous 'A'a, or 'A, was probably the first six-man racing canoe built in historic times. Weeks knew that the canoe had to be fast for paddling, but it also had to be serviceable for fishing, sailing and surfing.

It is interesting to note that until the turn of the century almost all canoe racing, either by sailing or paddling, was confined to people of Hawaiian ancestry. It was not until after 1900 that non-Hawaiians started paddling Hawaiian canoes. 1906 is the earliest date of record of information on a canoe race. It was also that year that Prince Kuhi'o first sent the 'A'a from Kona to Hono-lulu claiming that it was the "...most perfectly built and fastest racing canoe in Hawaii." As ten thousand spectators lined Honolulu Harbor, the 'A'a won the race by an incredible six lengths.

The sleek and beautiful 'A'a went on to win many more races. In 1910 Prince Kuhi'o retired the canoe from racing. He took it back to Kona where it was used for sailing, surfing and fishing. In 1923 the 'A'a was given to the Bernice Pauahi Bishop Museum where it is permanently displayed as part of the Kapi'olani-Kalani'ana'ole Collection.

Near the turn of the century Weeks de-

'A'A, PRINCE KUHI'O'S RACING CANOE
Miles Fry, artist
koa and wiliwili
39.9 inches (scale 1 inch = 1 foot)
collection of the artist
photograph by Alfredo Furelos
(see premiere edition, pages 61 and 87)

signed two pieces of furniture which would become his hallmark. In an effort to express his love for Hawaiian music Weeks designed and built two settees with back and arms patterned after clefs in musical notation. Fashioned from select, oversized pieces of *koa* with particularly beautiful graining and curl, these benches were perceived more as sculpture than as mere functional pieces of furniture. Acclaim for the work on these two pieces was immediate and widespread throughout the Kingdom. Queen Lili'uokalani displayed one in her home. One of the settees can still be seen today at Washington Place, now the home of Hawaii's Governor and Mrs. John D. Waihe'e.

Weeks' furniture business grew in the early 1900's. He was making regular furniture shipments to Honolulu. In spite of his success Weeks was always simply described as a 'carpenter' throughout his career. This misleading generalization somehow doesn't quite capture the essence and talent of this gifted gentleman.

Henry and Rebecca Weeks raised six children in Kainaliu. In 1912 Henry died at the age of seventy-six. He lived his last years with his oldest son William and daughter-in-law Betsy Ackerman Weeks. He is remembered by family members as a very proud man who inherited many of his father's English ways. One grand-daughter remembers her mother mentioning that Mr. Weeks never wanted to take his meals in the kitchen, preferring the dining room like all proper Englishmen.

The Weeks family homestead is still intact. As was the custom of the day, several family members are buried on the property, including Mr. Weeks. His beloved workshop is long since gone, replaced years ago by a flower garden. Many of his descendants still populate West Hawaii. The most memorable pieces of his legacy of beautiful woodwork hold places of honor at Hulihe'e Palace, the Bishop Museum and Washington Place.

(opposite left)
SETTEE
koa wood, 6 feet 4 inches long by 2 feet 4 inches wide by 3 feet 5 inches high (back)
collection of Pudding and Chuck Lassiter
photograph by Norman Makio

My great grandmother, Eliza Roy of Kainaliu, had commissioned Henry Weeks to make several of these koa settees. In our family I know of six others. He also made the straight back benches that had a covering of *lau hala* pillows on them. I recall as a child my grandmother had these in her living room for us to look at and not to sit on. In fact, we always sat on the floor because it made her feel better that we didn't get anything dirty. She and Betsy Weeks were most close. Back to great grandmother Roy, after she passed on my direct grandmother Lilinoe Roy Wall and grandfather Allan S. Wall opened up the first hotel in Kona, "Mahealani." Henry Weeks made rockers and other slat back pieces for the Roys. At that time the home where they lived had two of these settees in the living room. They were passed on to my mother Kapua Heuer. Currently, I have one of them and my sister the other.

-- PUDDING LASSITER
Papaikou, Hawaii

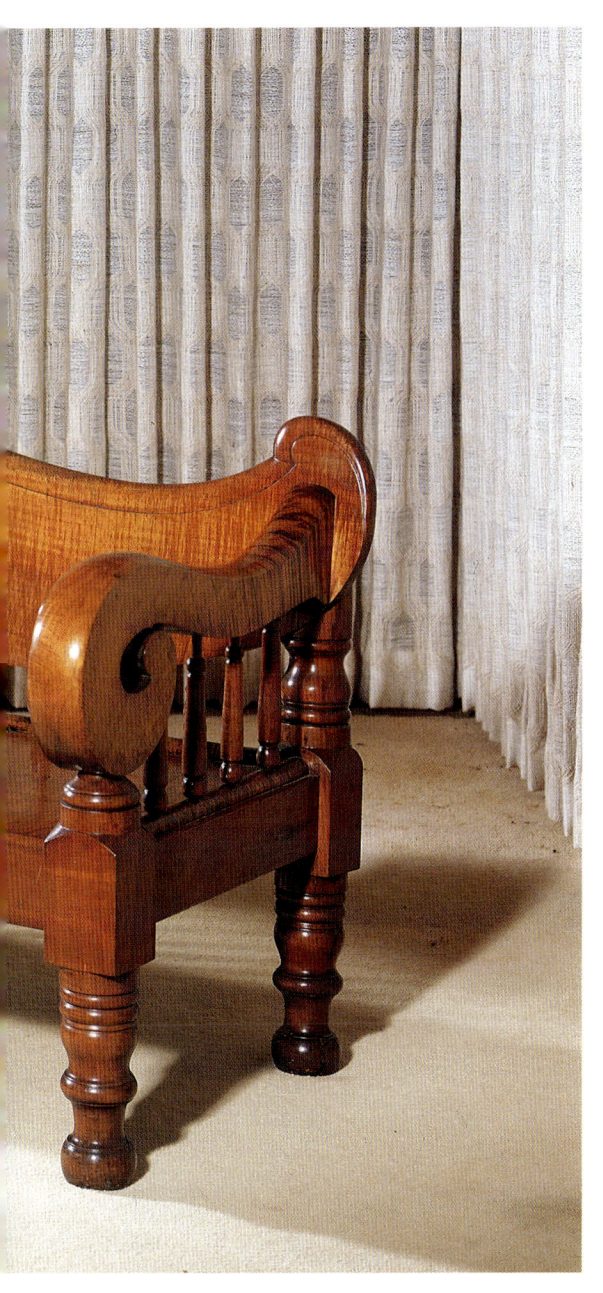

The Big Island of Hawaii takes pride in remembering one of her most outstanding professional woodworkers of Hawaiian ancestry, Henry Weeks, Jr.

-- REBECCA CROCKETT
Kailua-Kona, Hawaii

COVER ARTIST
SECOND EDITION

FUMIE BONK

FIRE BIRDS IN A FOREST
raku fired ceramic, 27 by 14 inches
photograph by Alfredo Furelos

COVER ARTIST
PREMIERE EDITION

EDGE OF GARDEN
oil on linen, 48 by 32 inches
photograph by Ed Gross

JOHN THOMAS

GALLERIES
OF HAWAII ISLAND

The Maya Gallery represents the work of distinguished fine artists from Hawaii, New York and Japan. Original works in various mediums are on display. Japanese Folk Art, antique Silk Kimono, handmade paper, jewelry and crafts by local artists are also displayed. There are frequent one man shows throughout the year.

ARTISTS: Hawaii - Satoru Abe (painting and sculpture), George Allen (painting), Henry Bianchini (bronze and wood sculpture), Tai Lake (fine woodwork), Tadashi Sato (painting), John Thomas (oil and watercolor painting), Fumie Bonk (pottery); New York - Herman Cherry (painting), Dorothy Dehner (etchings, watercolor, mixed media); Japan - Katsunori Hamanishi (mezzotint), and antique fine art and furniture pieces

MAYA GALLERY

Post Office Box 71
Kamuela, Hawaii 96743
phone 885-9633
DIRECTOR: Murthi Vinayaga
HOURS: 10am to 6pm daily
DIRECTIONS: at historic Hale Kea Ranch Estate on Kawaihae Road
PARKING: ample free parking
WHEELCHAIR ACCESS: yes, ramp with wheelchair entrance rear of gallery, ring doorbell for assistance
DINING: yes, at Hale Kea

SHOWCASE GALLERY

Post Office Box 4895
Kailua-Kona, Hawaii 96745-4895
phone 322-9711
DIRECTOR: Jean Josepho-Hamilton and Lynn Herron
HOURS: 9am to 6pm Mon - Sat
10am to 5pm Sun
DIRECTIONS: in Keauhou Shopping Village, Keauhou Resort
PARKING: ample free parking
WHEELCHAIR ACCESS: yes
DINING: yes, a variety of restaurants at Keauhou Shopping Village

The Showcase Gallery was established in 1981 in order to promote professional artists and craftsmen who have dedicated their careers to the pursuit of excellence and originality in their chosen field. The Gallery retails original paintings in a variety of mediums, contemporary handcrafted jewelry, handbuilt ceramics, art glass, baskets, wood, posters, limited edition prints and note cards.
ARTISTS: Joan Blackshear, Sue Clark, Ron Hamilton, Robert Joiner, Beth McCormick, Randy Morehouse, Phan Nguyen Barker, Karin Novak-Neal, Sandra Nelson, Arlene Nichols, Leah Niemoth, Jim Nottage, Jennifer Pontz

The Chocolate Orchid is a family owned and run multi-media gallery which features first and foremost the artists of the Big Island. We maintain high standards that contribute to the Gallery's reputation for integrity. We bring to you the work of the leading artists of Hawaii Island. Those artists featured at the Gallery rank among the very best on the Islands, and their artistic credentials have been well established in the market place of excellence. Stop by, say Hi! and browse through the Orchid Isle's largest selection of local art.

ARTISTS: Phan Barker, Ron Dalquist, Jane Davis, Digant, Lark Dimond-Cates, Gay Jensen, Robert Joiner, Herb Kane, Ina Koch, Mary Koski, Brad Lewis, Kathy Long, Miles Mason, Beth McCormick, Keith McGuire, James Morgan, Randy Morehousé, Jim Nottage, Karin Novak-Neal, Jennifer Pontz, Vicki Serva, Kristen Shaw, Linda & Larry Stevens, Janet Sorum, Lynn StAmand, Kim Starr, Budd Steinhilber, Sue Swerdlow, Diana Thanos, John Thomas, James Watt, Alexis Wilson

CHOCOLATE ORCHID GALLERY

75-5729 Alii Drive
Post Office Box 2926
Kailua-Kona, Hawaii 96745
phone 329-5548 and 329-1092
CONTACT PERSON: Dei Sluss
HOURS: 9am to 9pm Mon - Sat
12 noon to 9pm Sun
DIRECTIONS: in Kona Marketplace (old World Square Mall)
PARKING: convenient paid parking available in rear of Mall
WHEELCHAIR ACCESS: yes
DINING: variety of restaurants close by

THE ISLAND HERITAGE COLLECTION

Post Office Box 111333, Suite 132
Kamuela, Hawaii 96743
phone 885-2155
DIRECTOR: Marcia Goldman
HOURS: 10am to 8pm daily
DIRECTIONS: at historic Hale Kea Ranch Estate on Kawaihae Road
PARKING: ample free parking
WHEELCHAIR ACCESS: yes
DINING: yes, at Hale Kea

The Island Heritage Collection features the work of Hawaii's finest artists in limited edition lithograph/serigraphs, fine art posters and note cards. The intent of the gallery is to support the local art community while making fine art available and affordable to residents and visitors alike. Prints are available framed or unframed. We will gladly arrange for shipping anywhere in the world. In addition to prints we feature the lovely hand-blown art glass of Wilfred Yamazawa. We offer gift certificates in any denomination so your gift of art will always be perfect.
ARTISTS: Hawaii Island - Edwin Kayton, Mary Koski, James Morgan, Sunny Pauole, John Thomas; Hawaii State - Anthony Casay, Luigi Fumagalli, Richard Pettit, Rosalie Prussing, Marcia Ray, Gary Reed, Ari Vanderschoot and many others.

ARTISTS: painters- Marian Berger-Mahoney, Mary Koski, Kathy Long, Emrich Nicholson, Patrick Rankin, Janet Sorum, Kim Starr; hand crafts- Marcus Castaing, Pat Coito, Dan Cunningham, Dan DeLuz, Larry DeLuz, Mark Gardner, Beth McCormick, Tom Stoudt, Jack Straka, Hap Tahlman, David Tarleton, Jay Warner, Glenn Williams: fabrics- Nora Ofriel, Lauri Power, Suzanne Powers, Susun Schulze; glass- Jennifer Pontz, Gary Wagner; ceramics- Garron Alexander, Chiu Leong, Randy Morehouse; Rock carving- Rocky Asing

GALLERY OF GREAT THINGS

Post Office Box 6209
Kamuela, Hawaii 96743
phone 885-7706
DIRECTOR: Maria Brick
HOURS: 9am to 5pm Mon - Sat
Sun - call for info
DIRECTIONS: in Parker Square
PARKING: free parking in front or back
WHEELCHAIR ACCESS: yes
DINING: yes, at Parker Square

KAILUA VILLAGE ARTISTS GALLERY

Post Office Box 390887
Kailua-Kona, Hawaii 96739
phone 885-6789 ext. 7387
DIRECTOR: Felicia Fry
HOURS: 10am to 6pm daily
DIRECTIONS: Royal Waikoloan Hotel, Kohala Coast, first corridor to the right past Front Desk
PARKING: ample free parking
WHEELCHAIR ACCESS: yes
DINING: yes, in the Hotel

The Kailua Village Artists Gallery (KVA) is made up of artists living in the Kona area of Hawaii Island. Many of the artists had known each other and painted on location together for many years and exhibited their work wherever they could find space. They formed an association in April, 1985 and called themselves the Kailua Village Artists. In May, 1987 a space was found at the Royal Waikoloan Hotel and the KVA Gallery became a reality. Hawaiian culture, flowers, landscapes and seascapes are featured in the Gallery and members display their work in a professional manner. The artists themselves work in the Gallery and are able to offer their work at affordable prices. Artwork, which is also for sale, decorates the Royal Terrace Dining Room and the International Lounge at the end of the Waimea Wing of the mezzanine level at the Royal Waikoloan Hotel. ARTISTS: Mickle Beach, Penelope Culbertson, Bonnie Flint, Felicia Fry, Gay Jensen, Lorraine Jensen, Pat Mertens, Arlene Nichols, Budd Steinhilber, Jane Wilson, Norma DeGraff Wilson, Nancy Zufich

ART CENTERS
OF HAWAII ISLAND

sponsored by the UNIVERSITY OF HAWAII AT HILO

UNIVERSITY OF HAWAII AT HILO

Campus Center Gallery
Hilo, Hawaii 96720-4091
phone 933-3516 (Campus Center Information)
DIRECTOR: Professor Michael Marshall, Art Department
HOURS: 8am - 4:30pm Mon - Fri
ADMISSION: none
DIRECTIONS: from downtown Hilo take Kilauea Ave. or Kinoole St. inland to Kawili St., turn right, pass Kapiolani Street, turn right into Campus Center parking lot; Gallery located throughout third floor
PARKING: ample guest parking at Campus Center
WHEELCHAIR ACCESS: covered handicap parking, ramp to second floor, elevators
SHOP: none
DINING: cafeteria on first floor

above and opposite right
Campus Center Gallery, installation view of the 1990 Annual UHH Student Art Exhibition
photographs by Ken Banks, UHH Media Services

CAMPUS CENTER GALLERY

The Campus Center Gallery is a learning laboratory and visual resource benefitting students, the University and the community at large. Activities are performed on a voluntary basis by UHH Art Department faculty and students. A primary role of the Gallery is to function as a learning laboratory for the students. Gallery volunteers experience all phases pertaining to the organization and presentation of an art show. The exhibitions, in turn, provide a visual facet in the network of learning resources at the University of Hawaii at Hilo. The Annual UHH Student Art Show, held at the close of each academic year, is open to all students currently enrolled on any of the UHH campuses. All exhibitions and support for a

Permanent Collection of Prints and Drawings is assisted through funding provided by the UHH Student Activities Council. Typically, four exhibitions featuring printmaking, drawing and mixed media works on paper are mounted between September and May of each academic year. The presentations are a forum for mature and emerging younger artists of national and international reputation. For current listings of Gallery activities the public can contact the Campus Center Information desk.

THE ART DEPARTMENT

A major in Art is offered to students through a range of studio and history courses. Beginning with a foundation program in Beginning Drawing, Color Theory, 2-Dimensional and 3-Dimensional Design, more advanced courses are then offered in Drawing and Painting, Printmaking, Photography, Textiles/Fiber Arts, Ceramics and specialized Directed Studies. Offerings in the History of Art include, Western Art, Asian Art, Modern Art and the Art of China, Japan and Islam.

UNIVERSITY OF HAWAII AT HILO

The University of Hawaii at Hilo, with an enrollment of 4,000, is part of Hawaii's nine campus system of higher education. It currently incorporates the two-year Hawaii Community College with a four-year College of Arts and Sciences, a four-year College of Agriculture and a Center of Continuing Education and Community Service. In 1987 UHH-West Hawaii was established as an Outreach Higher Education Center of UHH. The educational philosophy of UHH is the development of the human potential to the fullest extent possible through an intellectually stimulating environment. Students may select from a variety of vocational and academic options: 24 certificate or associate degrees and 24 baccalaureate degrees in arts, agriculture, business administration and computer science.

HAWAII COMMUNITY COLLEGE

Hawaii Community College offers programs, courses and activities to fulfill the diverse educational, training and community needs of the residents of the Island as well as the State. Emphasis is placed on learning by involvement with the goal being for the student to gain skills and practical knowledge to find employment in his field of interest. A wide range of art courses are offered each semester with a number of classes held in conjunction with the Art Department. Students can earn Certificates of Achievement and Associate Degrees at the Community College.

CENTER FOR CONTINUING EDUCATION AND

above
Campus Center Gallery, installation view of the "Boy with Goldfish" exhibition of oil paintings and drawings by former visiting professor of Art John Thomas; this exhibition was co-sponsored by the Contemporary Art Center of Hawaii, the Honolulu Academy of Art and the State Foundation on Culture and the Arts as part of a State-wide tour with the Honolulu Symphony Orchestra performances of the "Boy with Goldfish" music
photograph by Linus Chao

COMMUNITY SERVICE

The Center for Continuing Education and Community Service (CCECS) serves as the outreach and extramural educational

above
the Campus Center building main entrance;
architect Takashi Anbe of Anbe, Aruga and
Ishizu; opened 1976
photograph by Linus Chao

arm of UHH. Classes are offered at population centers throughout Hawaii Island. CCECS offices are located on the Manono Street campus in Building 397 and at the UHH-West Hawaii Educational Center in Kealakekua, Kona. Courses in art and art history are offered every semester. Call the CCECS office at 933-3555 for information.

UHH WEST HAWAII

UHH West Hawaii has been a growing academic outreach center of UHH. It provides West Hawaii residents an opportunity to obtain appropriate courses leading to certificates, associate and baccalaureate degrees. Its major focus is the liberal arts undergraduate education and a select group of high quality professional and vocational programs. Located on the Kona Coast just off Highway 11 in Kealakekua the UHH-West campus overlooks the Kona coastline at the 1200 foot elevation. Established as an Educational Outreach Center in 1987, UHH-West offers an average of 38 courses per semester, including courses in the Visual Arts. Instructors are highly qualified full and part-time faculty recognized as experts in their fields, most holding advanced degrees. The UHH-West Library provides a growing collection of books, journals, videotapes, maps and reference materials.

sponsored by THE FRIENDS OF THE ARTS

THE WAILOA CENTER

Post Office Box 936, Hilo, Hawaii 96720
phone 933-4360
DIRECTOR: Pudding Lassiter
HOURS: 8am to 4:30pm Mon, Tues, Thurs, Fri; 12 to 8:30pm Wed; 9am to 3pm Sat
ADMISSION: none
DIRECTIONS: on Pauahi Street one-half block from Kamehameha Avenue; sign on left marks entrance road to Wailoa State Park and the Center
PARKING: ample parking by the Center
WHEELCHAIR ACCESS: yes
SHOP: none
DINING: picnicking on ground floor and nearby park

The gracefully-shaped building, designed by the Hilo firm of Oda - McCarty Architects Ltd, has been a gathering place for Island art, history and cultural activities since the early 1970s. The main gallery on the second floor was designed for major exhibitions and provides ample wall and floor space for installing two dimensional art and free standing pieces. Since September, 1986 the Center has continued to support the activities of the arts and culture of the community under the direction of Pudding Lassiter. She has created the Mini Fountain Gallery located on the ground floor. "Artists need this space for smaller solo shows and is another area for the public to enjoy," says Mrs. Lassiter. The Wailoa Center maintains rotating displays of Island artists' work in exhibition booths at the Hilo and Kona airports. Call for information on current shows and activities.

sponsored by THE FRIENDS OF THE ARTS

THE LYMAN HOUSE MEMORIAL MUSEUM

The Lyman House Memorial Museum is housed in two buildings -- the Lyman House, built in 1839 by the Reverend David and Sarah Lyman, and the Museum building added to the property in 1973. The Museum and Mission House provide fascinating and informative basic study of the Island and its past. The Museum houses a public collection of many of the most important 19th and early 20th century artists to have worked in Hawaii. This exhibit, "Kaha Ki'i 'o Hawai'i," is on the second floor at the top of the stairs. Also on public view is "The Shipman Foundation's Gallery of Chinese Art" displaying pieces from eight dynasties. Scholars are encouraged to do individual research at the Museum and House. Call for information on upcoming programs and lectures.

276 Haili Street, Hilo, Hawaii 96720
phone 935-5021
DIRECTOR: Dr. Leon H Bruno
HOURS: 9am to 5pm Mon - Sat
ADMISSION: $3.50 adults, $2.50 senior citizens over 60, children under 6 free, age 6 to 12 $1.50, age 13 to 18 $2.50
DIRECTIONS: from downtown Hilo up Haili Street 5 blocks
PARKING: 2-hour parking on Haili Street
WHEELCHAIR ACCESS: no access to Mission House, call for access to Museum
SHOP: gift shop in lobby
DINING: no dining facilities
TOURS: self-guided in Museum; interpreters at Mission House lead tours daily

sponsored by THE FRIENDS OF THE ARTS

THE CENTER

East Hawaii Cultural Council
Post Office Box 1312, Hilo, Hawaii 96721
phone 961-5711
DIRECTOR: Frances C. Sherrard
GALLERY DIRECTOR: Leila Mehle
HOURS: 9am to 4pm Mon - Sat
ADMISSION: none
DIRECTIONS: 141 Kalakaua Street
PARKING: metered parking on street
WHEELCHAIR ACCESS: ramp on inland side of Gallery building
SHOP: gift shop sells art objects and fine arts cards
DINING: picnicking across the street in Kalakaua Park

Located in the old Police Station in historic downtown Hilo, The Center is continually presenting exhibitions of Hawaii Island visual artists. The East Hawaii Cultural Council, the Center's parent organization, had its beginnings in 1967. The Center Gallery was opened in 1987. Exhibitions have featured group multi-media presentations with specific themes. Accompanying these exhibitions are related programs such as slide presentations, lectures, workshops and demonstrations. Heritage exhibitions with participation from community groups and individuals have also been a part of the activities. The second floor houses a space for performing arts presentations and will eventually accommodate a conference room, a small library, and even a little cafe.

sponsored by THE FRIENDS OF THE ARTS

The Volcano Art Center, with the cooperation of the National Park Service, was established in 1974 as a nonprofit educational and cultural organization. The Center is housed in an historical 1877 building which was originally used as a hostelry and built to replace a grass structure. In 1921 the building was moved from the crater edge to its present site. The gallery currently exhibits work by professional local artists. A spectrum of works in various mediums are always on view, and there is an ongoing schedule of one man shows. The Center's programming focus is in four major areas: visual arts, performing arts, literary arts and traditional Hawaiian culture. Classes, workshops, seminars, demonstrations, residencies, performances and exhibitions enhance public awareness and appreciation in each of these four areas. Call for information on the Center's current exhibition and activities schedule.

THE VOLCANO ART CENTER

Post Office Box 104
Hawaii National Park, Hawaii 96718-0104
phone 967-8222
EXECUTIVE DIRECTOR: John Campbell
GALLERY DIRECTOR: Audrey Forcier
HOURS: 9am to 6pm daily
ADMISSION: none
DIRECTIONS: located in Hawaii Volcanoes National Park next to the Visitor Center; take path to the left for 100 yards
PARKING: parking at the Visitor Center
WHEELCHAIR ACCESS: yes
SHOP: extensive selection of Hawaii Island crafts, books, note cards, posters, fabrics and apparel
DINING: breakfast, lunch and dinner at the Volcano House Lodge; picnicking welcome in Park

sponsored by THE FRIENDS OF THE ARTS

PAHOA ARTS AND CRAFTS GUILD

Post Office Box 1514, Pahoa, Hawaii 96778
phone 965-7335
DIRECTOR: Kent Canington
HOURS: 9:30am to 5:30pm daily
ADMISSION: none
DIRECTIONS: on the boardwalk in historic Pahoa
PARKING: ample free parking on the street
WHEELCHAIR ACCESS: call for access
SHOP: extensive selection of art and crafts
DINING: variety of restaurants nearby

The Pahoa Arts and Crafts Guild is a non-profit organization which is solely directed and run by its artist members. We feature artists in continuous shows at the Upstairs Gallery and showcase all of our members throughout the remaining area. The Guild holds workshops and demonstrations. Call for schedule information.
ARTISTS: Kent Canington, Sharon Carson, Linda Cerny, Suzanne Hall, K. T. Harrison, Beatrice Hoagland, Avi Kiriaty, Brad Lewis, Alan Liebensperger, Mango, Kimberly Parrish, Ana Reinhardt, Joe and Penny Shaver, Sara Steiner-Jackson, Eric Sumner, Barry Wilkenson, Erna Woo, Carlo Yamashita

sponsored by THE FRIENDS OF THE ARTS

The Waimea Art Center Gallery has been in existence since 1981 and is under the aegis of the Waimea Arts Council. Housed in the converted Fire Station, built in 1927, the Gallery schedules solo exhibitions ten months of the year. Two juried shows round out the year, "Na 'Opio" for children in May and the "Helen M. Cassidy Memorial Exhibition" for members of the Arts Council in October. Over 35 artists from north Hawaii have had solo shows at the Gallery. Just inside the front door of the Gallery is the Makali'i Room which shows a constantly changing selection of work by member artists. The public can be assured of meeting these artists as they frequently tend the Gallery.

THE WAIMEA ART CENTER

The Waimea Arts Council
Post Office Box 1818
Kamuela, Hawaii 96743
phone 885-6109
GALLERY CHAIRMAN: Robert Althouse
HOURS: Tues, Thurs, Sat 10am to 2pm
ADMISSION: none
DIRECTIONS: in old Waimea Fire Station, southwest corner at the traffic light
PARKING: on the street
WHEELCHAIR ACCESS: yes, level
SHOP: works on display are for sale
DINING: numerous nearby restaurants

sponsored by THE FRIENDS OF THE ARTS

KAHILU THEATRE

Kahilu Theatre Foundation
Post Office Box 549
Kamuela, Hawaii 96743
phone 885-6017
DIRECTOR: Virginia C. Pfaff
HOURS: 9am to 5pm Mon - Fri; call box office for schedule of exhibitions, performances and summer classes
ADMISSION: for performances
DIRECTIONS: at traffic light in Waimea behind bank building through parking lot, entrance on Mauna Kea side
PARKING: plentiful
WHEELCHAIR ACCESS: ramp on east side
SHOP: none
DINING: numerous nearby restaurants
TOURS: phone box office to make arrangements for a tour

The new Kahilu Theatre building, completed in 1981, is a center for cultural activities in the Waimea Community. Designed by Wimberly, Whisenand, Allison, Tong and Goo Inc., and funded by Richard Smart, a spacious gallery area to the left in the Theatre lobby hosts substantial shows of local visual artists. These art exhibitions accompany performances in the auditorium during the September through April season. Arts education is an important part of the Foundation's thrust. The "Summer Arts" program provides classes in art, drama and music for the community. The Kahilu Theatre Foundation's 1990-1991 season marks its eleventh anniversary. Managing Director since 1984, Virginia Pfaff came to the Kahilu Theatre after extensive Mainland experience at Wolftrap, the Cleveland Playhouse Square, and the Victory Theatre in Dayton. For more information regarding exhibitions, performances and classes contact the Theatre.

sponsored by THE FRIENDS OF THE ARTS

SKEA is a non-profit community organization dedicated to providing cultural and educational activities to the rural South Kona community. Hula, judo, art and dance workshops, a working pottery studio and a preschool are some of the ongoing activities. Twice a year the volunteer organization mounts a major art exhibit of local talent, complete with festivities -- the Annual Art Show weekend in February and Art Expo, a children's art exhibit in May. Their latest project has been the formation of an artists' cooperative which runs a gallery and gift shop on the grounds and features the work of local artists in many mediums. Call for current activities information.

COTTAGE GALLERY

South Kona Educational Association (SKEA)
Post Office Box 256
Honaunau, Hawaii 96726
phone 328-9392
ADMINISTRATOR: Susan Rice
HOURS: 9:30am to 5pm daily
ADMISSION: none
DIRECTIONS: Mamalahoa Hwy. (Route 11) one mile south of Honaunau School and mile past the "106 mile" marker
PARKING: ample parking in front or behind the Gallery
WHEELCHAIR ACCESS: yes Gallery and grounds, main building has stairs
SHOP: the Cottage Gallery sells art objects and gift items, staffed by participating artists
DINING: picnic tables in the yard except on Tues - Thurs am

sponsored by THE FRIENDS OF THE ARTS

THE HULIHE'E PALACE MUSEUM

75-5718 Alii Drive
Kailua-Kona, Hawaii 96740
phone 329-1877
DIRECTOR: Fanny Collins Au Hoy
HOURS: 9am to 4pm daily
ADMISSION: $4.00 adults, $3.00 senior citizens over 65, $1.00 students 11 - 18, 50¢ children
DIRECTIONS: center of Kailua village across from the Mokuaikaua Church
PARKING: in municipal parking lot block inland
WHEELCHAIR ACCESS: limited
SHOP: Gift Shop on property
DINING: facility available for select functions
TOURS: continuous all day

Built in 1838 by Governor John Adams Kuakini, Hulihe'e Palace remained until 1916 a vacation spa for Hawaiian royalty. The historic two-story structure, now a museum, displays a collection of furniture and effects of Hawaiian royalty, including furniture pieces by Kona master woodworker Henry Weeks [see pages 79 to 83], as well as ancient artifacts owned and maintained by the Daughters of Hawaii. Majestically surrounded by an expanse of lawn and trees, Hulihe'e Palace stands on the shores of Kailua Bay in verdant Kona.

sponsored by THE FRIENDS OF THE ARTS

The West Hawaii Gallery, located in the lobby of the Keauhou Beach Hotel, is a home for many Kona area artists and crafts people. The Gallery serves as an extension and retail outlet for members of the West Hawaii Arts Guild and is a cooperative project of the Guild and the Keauhou Beach Hotel. On rotating display are general membership shows including paintings in oil, watercolor and acrylic; photography; wall hangings in weaving, batik and fiber; sculpture in a variety of mediums including wood, metal and stone; ceramics, glass, jewelry; one-of-a-kind apparel and other unique objects. The Gallery is representative of a broad sweep of talent designed to suit every taste. The public is invited to enjoy a friendly atmosphere and meet the artists of West Hawaii who are attending the Gallery. Call for current exhibition information.

WEST HAWAII GALLERY

West Hawaii Arts Guild
Keauhou Beach Hotel
78-6740 Alii Drive
Kailua-Kona, Hawaii 96740
phone 322-3441
PRESIDENT: Lee Palakiko
HOURS: 10am to 6pm Mon - Thurs
10am to 9pm Fri - Sun
ADMISSION: none
DIRECTIONS: at the Keauhou Beach Hotel on the ground floor near lobby
PARKING: ample free parking
WHEELCHAIR ACCESS: yes, ramp on inland side
SHOP: fine art, wearable art and crafts, all by West Hawaii artists
DINING: dining at the Hotel

FRIENDS OF THE ARTS

HAWAII TROPICAL BOTANICAL GARDEN
Explore 17 acres of beautiful Hawaiian rain forest with over 1,600 varieties of tropical plants. Enjoy waterfalls and the spectacular beauty of this unique garden in a valley by the ocean. Located on the 4-mile scenic route 7 miles north of Hilo. A Nature lover's and photographer's paradise. Acclaimed to be the most beautiful area in Hawaii.
a non-profit foundation nature preserve
P O Box 1415 • Hilo, Hawaii 96721 • 964-5233

featuring
French Creole Cuisine
in an elegant
turn of the century building
in historic
Downtown Hilo

**serving Dinner
seven nights a week
Reservations: 935-5111**

ROUSSELS
60 KEAWE STREET • HILO, HAWAII 96720

Tropical Dreams ™

creators of fine Macadamia products
and exquisite Ice Creams & Sorbets,
is pleased to lend support and
encouragement to Malama Arts for
their commitment in bringing Hawaii
Island artists to the fore.

**Tropical Dreams Gourmet Shoppe
Sakamoto Building
Kapaau, Hawaii 96755 • 889-6295**

COLORS OF HAWAII

Kona's supermarket of printing services
computer typesetting • graphics • darkroom
single color • multi color • full color process printing
bindery • laminating up to 24 inches wide
3 - 4 day delivery on most orders

74-5543 #4 Kaiwi Street • Kailua-Kona, Hawaii 96740 • 326-1000

BEST WISHES TO ALL OF THE FINE ARTIST FEATURED HERE!

Martin & MacArthur

a tradition in Hawaii for over 25 years, offers heirloom quality handcrafted furniture, uncommon gift items and custom picture framing. The showroom at Davies Pacific Center regularly features the work of some of Hawaii's most noted artists including Jack Straka, Jay Warner and Beth McCormick.

**831 Bishop Street Ste 131
Honolulu, Hawaii 96813 • 524-4434**

---

kona FRAME shop

Established in 1976

WITH AN EMPHASIS ON
quality workmanship • service
innovative design
specializing in
archival and conservation framing
Poster gallery • Koa wood frames

**74-5484 Kaiwi Street • Kailua-Kona
Hawaii 96740 • 329-1722**

CAPRICORN BOOKSHOP

a full-line bookstore serving Hamakua and North and South Kohala
Books • Cards • Gift Items • We rent Lazaris Videos
located at the Waimea Center

P O Box 2166 • Kamuela, Hawaii 96743 • 885-0039

cabinets
kitchen design
Kolbe & Kolbe
wood windows and doors
CLEMMER & CLEMMER
PRECISION WOOD WORKS INC.

**73-4820 Kanalani Street, Bay 12
Kailua Kona, Hawaii 96740
329-3088 • FAX 326-5480**

In appreciation of the art community of Kona, we congratulate you! At Insurance Hawaii, like artists, we take pride in our profession. Come in and meet our creative insurance artists.
Serving Hawaii over 45 years.
HOME • AUTO • BUSINESS

**75-167E Hualalai Road, Ste 1
Kailua-Kona, Hawaii 96740
Kona 329-4844 • Waimea 885-7717**

JERRÉ TANNER MUSIC STUDIO

Hawaiian Classical Music for your video and film • a sensuous orchestral sound created using state-of-the-art computer directed synthesis • extensive library of new arrangements of traditional Hawaiian music as well as sensational original compositions • SMPTE compatible.

P O Box 1478 • Kailua-Kona, Hawaii 96745 • 329-5828

KONA FAMILY YMCA

promotes
Good Health
Strong Families
Confident Kids
Quality Communities
and a
Better World

329-YMCA

sponsored by Mike and Beth Kasser

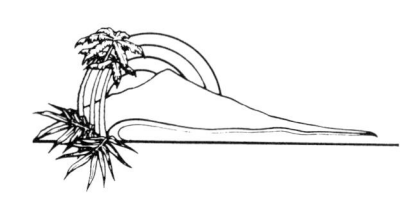

RAINBOW ADVERTISING

advertising and promotions including photography, specialty items, post cards business cards, brochures and catalog pages
AUDIO & VISUAL MARKETING CONCEPTS

165 Wilder Road • Hilo, Hawaii 96720 • 969-9968 or 935-7831

Mauna Loa Macadamia Nut

Visitor Center

OPEN DAILY
8:30 am - 5 pm
admission is free
near Hilo, on the Big Island of Hawaii

H. C. 01 Box 3
Hilo, Hawaii 96720
966-8612

Cunningham Gallery
116 KEAWE ST. • 935-7223

print & poster gallery
FEATURING ARTISTS OF HAWAII

full service custom picture framing
Traditional to Contemporary
Acrylic boxes and Displays

116 Keawe Street • Hilo, Hawaii
96720 935-9122 or 935-7223

HAWAIIAN CLASSICAL MUSIC

compositions by Jerré Tanner,
Hawaii's leading symphonic and
operatic composer
now available on stereo cassette
BOY WITH GOLDFISH • London
Symphony Orchestra (HCMS001)
HAWAIIAN CLASSICAL MUSIC
(HCMS002)
order direct from
**Multi-Arts Inc. • P O Box 1478
Kailua-Kona, Hawaii 96745
329-5828**

ISLAND ENERGY SYSTEMS

has focused on two goals -- saving
money for Hawaii's business and
preserving our Islands' fragile energy
resources -- utilizing progressive
energy conservation technology to
improve efficiency and reduce
energy costs.

Joseph Petrie, President
P O Box 316 • Paauilo, Hawaii
96776 • 776-1333

NORTH HAWAII COMMUNITY HOSPITAL, INC.

The goal of North Hawaii Community Hospital, Inc. is to provide accessible acute care hospital services to the residents and visitors of North Hawaii, and to actively involve individuals and families in their own health in order to maximize resources and ensure overall excellence in health care.

P O Box 2799 • Kamuela, Hawaii 96743 • 885-2722
sponsored by William N. and Kathleen C. Jardine

THE HENRY OPUKAHAIA SCHOOL

thoroughly Christian atmosphere
strong academics
well-qualified faculty
interscholastic athletics
boarding (grades 5-12 Keaau)
As we enter our 20th year we are the fastest growing private shool in Hawaii today.

**Three locations • Keaau 966-9321
Kona 329-1614 • Kohala 889-0502**

sponsored by Kai Markell, III

Valley Interiors

Floor Covering
Window Treatments
Wall Paper
Interior Designs
Fuller O'Brien Paints

*residential • commercial
institutional*

74-5599 Luhia Street
Kailua-Kona, Hawaii 96740
329-2067

HAWAII PREPARATORY ACADEMY

Offering a unique educational experience for day and boarding students from kindergarten through grade 12. Campuses in Kamuela and Kona on the Island of Hawaii.

P O Box 428 • Kamuela, Hawaii 96743 • 885-7321

sponsored by Putman D. Clark

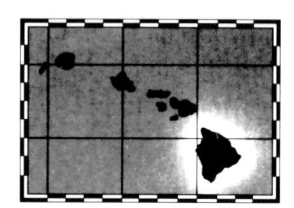

B·I·G
BIG ISLAND GROUP

The Big Island Group is proud to support our Island's multi-talented visual artists who help make Hawaii a very rich and special place.

**HC02 Box 5900 • Kohala Coast,
Hawaii 96743 • 885-5900**

sponsored by Malama Arts Inc.

The Family Crisis Shelter, Inc.

Call our 24 hour crisis and information line.
All calls confidential.

West Hawaii	East Hawaii
322-2799	959-8400
322-SAFE	959-5825

"Never another battered person"

sponsored by Lisa Clark

DESTINATION HILO

Sunrise in Hilo is a quiet celebration of life. Each day another symphony of Nature is played before an audience of warm, friendly people. Ah ... peaceful Hilo mornings are what paradise is meant to be.

P O Box 1391 • Hilo, Hawaii 96720 • 935-5294

Destination: KONA COAST

The Last and the Best of Hawaii for everyone to enjoy. Our soft sunsets are a perfect ending to each smooth day of exploration and discovery. Celebrate your sublimest self on the ancient playground of Hawaiian Royalty ... *E Komo Mai!* The Historic Kona Coast welcomes you.

P O Box 3210 • Kailua-Kona Hawaii 96745 • 329-1901

KONA HISTORICAL SOCIETY
museum hours
Tues - Fri 9:00 am - 3:00 pm
Saturdays 9:00 am - 12:00 noon
closed all holidays
admission by donation
research facilities
library and manuscript collection
photograph and artifact collection
open by appointment only
Post Office Box 398 • Captain Cook Hawaii 96704 • 323-3222
sponsored by Ahlo & Associates Inc.

MALAMA ARTS INC.

continues a ten-year tradition of publishing and distributing state-wide Hawaii Island artists in fine art books, limited edition serigraphs, prints and posters. Our HAWAII MASTERS SERIES fine arts note cards are available at galleries and gift shops throughout Hawaii.

P O Box 1478 • Kailua-Kona Hawaii 96745 • 329-5828

WEST HAWAII ARTS GUILD

offers to its members and the West Hawaii community the opportunity to enrich our lives through art. The Guild is dedicated to fulfilling the current arts needs of the community as well as providing the leadership in developing West Hawaii as a future world-class arts destination.

P O Box 3386 • Kailua-Kona, Hawaii 96745 • 324-1349

ARTISTS INDEX

INDEX KEY
artist name   district
principal medium - specific mediums
galleries
GALLERY KEY
Art Mart - Art Mart of Kona
Center - The Center (EHCC)
Choc Orch - Chocolate Orchid Gallery
Cott Gal - Cottage Gallery (SKEA)
Cunningham - Cunningham Gallery
Fiberarts - Fiberarts/Topstitch
Gal Gt Things - Gallery of Great Things
Isl Heritage - Island Heritage Gallery
KVA Gal - Kailua Village Artists Gallery
Loyd's - Loyd's Art Supply
Mart & MacA - Martin & MacArthur
MKBH Gal - Mauna Kea Beach Hotel Gallery
Maya - Maya Gallery
Pahoa - Pahoa Arts and Crafts Gallery
Reyn - Reyn Spooner Inc.
Showcase - the Showcase Gallery
VAC - Volcano Art Center
WAC - Waimea Art Center
Waimea Gen St - Waimea General Store

ACKERMAN, GARY   Kohala
painting - oil, acrylic, watercolor

ADAMS, LISA   Kona
crafts - porcelain, graphics, computer graphics
Cott Gal

ADDLESBERGER, DALE   Kona
painting - oil, watercolor

AEHEGMA, AELBERT   Kau
sculpture - oil

AH SING, ROCKY   Waimea
sculpture - lava rock
Gal Gt Things

AHIA, CHRISTINE   Hilo
textiles - fabrics, wearable art, quilts
VAC
featured artist, 2nd edition

AINSWORTH, CAROLYN   Waimea
textiles - batik, clothes design

ALEXANDER, GARRON   Volcano
crafts - ceramics
Gal Gt things, VAC
featured artist, 2nd edition

ALLEN, CHRISTOPHER   Puna
crafts - woodworker

ALMONTE, EDWARD   Kona
painting - acrylic, oil

ALTHOUSE, ROBERT   Waimea
painting - oil, acrylic, pastel
Center, WAC

AMEMIYA, CLAYTON   Hilo
crafts - ceramics
featured artist, premiere edition

ANDERSON, DAVID   Hamakua
crafts - furniture maker
featured artist, 2nd edition

ANDERSON, GAYLE   Kona
painting - collage, tempera, watercolor
Gal Gt Things, VAC
featured artist, premiere edition

ANON   Puna
painting - watercolor, oil, graphics

ARAGON, MARGIE   Puna
painting - watercolor, acrylics, air brush

AUSTIN, EDWARD   Kohala
painting - watercolor, oil
MKBH Gal

AYERS, KATHERINE   Kona
painting - pastel, charcoal, watercolor, oil

BALAI, SHARON   Waimea
crafts - Hawaiian quilting
Fiberarts
featured artist, premiere & 2nd edition

BARBOSA, RON   Kona
sculpture - traditional Hawaiian wood carving

BARGE, MILLIE   Hamakua
painting

BARTMAN, C BART   Kona
crafts - Furniture Making

BARTON, PAM   Volcano
crafts - ceramics, fiber
VAC

BATES, GAIL   Waimea
crafts
Gal Gt Things

BEACH, MICKLE   Kona
painting - oil
KVA Gal
featured artist, premiere edition

BEATTIE, ELSIE   Puna
painting - watercolor, acrylic, fabric, collage

BELCHER, BOBBIE   Hilo
painting - oil, watercolor, ceramics, photography

BELSKI, TOMAS Hilo
painting - pen & ink

BEN, GERALD Kona
crafts - ceramics, raku, wood, furniture

BERGER-MAHONEY, MARIAN Volcano
painting
Cunningham, Gal Gt Things
featured artist, 2nd edition

BEVER, DAVID Kona
crafts - stained & fused glass, koa woodwork

BEYER, HUNTER Volcano
painting - pen and ink
Fiberarts

BHAVA Puna
painting - Pencil Color & Lead

BIANCHINI, HENRY Puna
sculpture - bronze, wood
Maya

BLACKSHEAR, JOAN Kona
textiles - hand painted silk, garments, wall pieces
Lyman House Museum, Showcase, Viviana Boutique
featured artist, premiere edition

BLACKWELL, PETER Kona
crafts - furniture making
featured artist, 2nd edition

BOCKUS, ROGER Kona
painting - watercolor

BOGNER, WES Kau
painting - acrylic
featured artist, premiere edition

BONK, FUMI Waimea
crafts - ceramics
Maya
cover artist, 2nd edition

BONK, SANDY Puna
crafts

BREESE-RABIN, TEUNISSE Kona
crafts - ceramics, porcelain, stoneware, raku
Cott Gal, VAC
featured artist, 2nd edition

BROENNIMANN, ANITA Kona
painting - watercolor, acrylic, batik

BROENNIMANN, ERICH Kona
sculpture - wood, stone, bronze

CARROLL, CAROL Kona
crafts - porcelain, stoneware
Cott Gal

CARSON, SHARON Puna
painting - watercolor, oil, acrylic, batik

CASTAING, MARCUS Kau
crafts - furniture
Gal Gt Things, Mart & MacA

CHAO, JANE Hilo
painting - silk painting
Cunningham Gal

CHAO, LINUS Hilo
painting - watercolor, caligraphy, photog, cinema
Cunningham Gal
featured artist, 2nd edition

CHAPON, DEE Kohala
crafts - ceramics
Gal Gt Things

CHARON, KEN Puna
painting - acrylic, pen & ink, wood sculpture
VAC

CHEN, EDDY Hilo
painting

CHENINA Hilo
misc - mixed media

CHING, BRUCE Puna
crafts - wood working

CLARK, SUSAN Puna
painting - oil
Gal Gt Things
Showcase, VAC

COITO sr, PATRICK Hamakua
crafts - bowls, placks & trophies
Gal Gt Things

COLEMAN, S E Kona
painting - mixed media, performance art

COOK, PI'ILANI Hilo
painting - watercolor
Gal Gt Things

CROCKER, ELLEN Kona
painting - watercolor
featured artist, premiere edition

CULBERTSON, KIMBERLY Kona
painting - watercolor

CULBERTSON, PENELOPE Kona
painting - watercolor
KVA Gal

CUNNINGHAM, DAN Waimea
crafts - bowl turning
Gal Gt Things

CUNNINGHAM, SHIRLEY Kona
painting - oil, acrylic

DARR, EVA LIN Hilo
painting - watercolor, ink, acrylic

DATSON, BETSY Kona
crafts - basketry

DAVID, REGINALD Kona
photography
Rana Productions

DE LUZ, DAN Hilo
crafts - wood working
Gal Gt Things
featured artist, 2nd edition

DE LUZ, LARRY Hilo
crafts - wood working
Gal Gt Things

DEVINS, JEFF Waimea
graphics - pen & ink, acrylics

DIGANT Kohala
painting - watercolor
Choc Orch

DIMOND-CATES, LARK Kona
painting - watercolor
Choc Orch

DOUGLAS, LORN Kau
crafts - wood working
Mart & MacA

DUNN, KELLY Kohala
crafts - wood working
Mart & MacA

DRUNSIC, THALIA Kona
photography

EHU, BETH Hilo
crafts
Hawaiian quilting

EPPERSON, DON Puna
painting - acrylic
VAC

FAIRCHILD, RICHARD Puna
photography

FELLERMAN, JANE Kona
painting - oil

FIELDS, LARRY Puna
crafts - wood working

FLINT, BONNIE Kona
painting - acrylic
KVA Gal

FRENCH, PETER Waimea
photography
Peter French Studio
featured artist, premiere edition

FRY, FELICIA Kona
painting - mixed media
KVA Gal

FRY, MILES Kona
crafts - woodworking, ship models
featured artist, premiere edition

FURELOS, ALFREDO Waimea
photography
Alfredo's Photo Studio
featured artist, 2nd edition

GAIL, JANICE Hamakua
painting - oil, pastel, watercolor
WAC

GARDNER, BARBARA Waimea
textiles - gouache on paper, fabric design
Reyn
featured artist, 2nd edition

GARDNER, MARK Kau
crafts - wood working
Gal Gt Things

GEPHART, PAUL Hamakua
sculpture - island woods, seed jewelry

GHEN, KAREN Puna
painting

GIACOMETTI, GRETCHEN Kona
painting - watercolor

GIMBEL, SAM Hamakua
painting

GINN, ELIZABETH Kona
painting - watercolor, silk, wearable art
Reyn

GOMES, DAVID Kohala
crafts - guitars, ukuleles
featured artist, premiere & 2nd edition

GREEN, PUA Waimea
textiles - wearable art, accessories

GREEN, YUKO Waimea
painting - pen & ink, pencil, watercolor

GREENE, SHARON Hilo
painting - watercolor, acrylic, photography

GREENFELD, CAROLYN Kona
painting - oil, paper

GROSS, ED Kona
photography
Images Photography

GROWNEY, JAMES Waimea
painting

GUALTIERI, EMILY Kona
crafts - jewelry
Choc Orch

GUNTER, GARRISON Kona
painting - acrylic, print making
WAC

GUNTHER, ERIK Hamakua
crafts - wood working
Fiberarts

HAFNER, CRISTINE Waimea
graphics - graphic design

HAGAN, HANNA Kona
crafts - ceramics, marble carving
Gal Gt Things

HALL, PAT Waimea
painting - watercolor, drawing
Gal Gt Things

HALL, SUZANNE Puna
painting - oil, pastel, mixed media
Pahoa

HAMILTON, RON Kona
crafts - furniture
Showcase

HAMPTON, JOE Hamakua
painting - mixed media

HANAPE, ALAPAI Puna
sculpture - wood

HANCOCK, JUDY Waimea
crafts - jewelry
Gal Gt Things

HARRISON, ANN Waimea
graphics - interior design

HARVEY, D E Kona
painting - air brush, organic pigments in water

HASHIMOTO, CALVIN Kona
sculpture - wood

HAYLEY, MICHAEL Hilo
graphics - serigraph, oil, watercolor, color pencil

HENNES, JOANNE Kona
painting - oil, watercolor
featured artist, premiere & 2nd edition

HICKS, STEPHEN Waimea
crafts - furniture
featured artist, premiere edition

HILL, ELIZABETH Kona
graphics - interior design, pastel, pencil, charcoal

HIRLEMAN, DON Hilo
painting - watercolor

HODSON, MELITTA Kona
misc - interior design, art glass, plaster

HOY, MARGARET Kohala
painting

HYDE, DOROTHEA Kona
painting

INNOCENTI, KRISTEN Kona
painting - watercolor, acrylic

IRA, S M Kona
painting - watercolor, oil, paper

IRVINE, STEVE Puna
painting - mixed media

IRWIN, BILL Puna
crafts - glass

IZUMI, JASON Kona
painting - watercolor, acrylic
featured artist, 2nd edition

JA-TANAKA, ANNE Kona
painting - watercolor

JENSEN, GAY Kona
painting - watercolor, pastels
Choc Orch, KVA Gal

JENSEN, LORRAINE Kona
painting - watercolor, pastel, mixed media
KVA Gal

JENSEN, ROBIN Waimea
crafts - Hawaiian quilting

JOHNSEN, DENISE Hamakua
painting - watercolor, acrylic, pencil

JOHNSEN, ERIC Hamakua
crafts - furniture

JOHNSON, JACQUELYN Waimea
painting - watercolor, oil

JOHNSON, SANDRA Hilo
painting

JOINER, ROBERT Puna
crafts - ceramics
Choc Orch, Showcase

JUAN, DEBRA Waimea
crafts - fibers
Fiberarts

KAGELER, DINA Volcano
photography

KAHN, AZURA Puna
painting - watercolor

KAIAMA, TSUGI Waimea
crafts - featherwork
featured artist, premiere & 2nd edition

KALALANI Kohala
crafts - Hawaiian quilting

KALAUOKAAEA, CATHY Kona
painting - watercolor, collage, acrylic

KAM, KATHLEEN Puna
painting - oil, acrylic, watercolor, colored pencil

KANE, HERB Kona
painting - oil, graphics, sculpture
Choc Orch, Cunningham

KAPVAL, TIM Hilo
crafts - ceramics

KAUHANE, GAIL Volcano
painting - oil, watercolor, pastel
VAC

KAWAMURA, JAMES Puna
painting - oil

KAYTON, EDWIN Kona
painting - oil, sculpture
Isl Heritage
featured artist, premiere & 2nd edition

KIRIATY, AVRAHAM Puna
painting
oil, prints, lava sculpture
Pahoa, VAC

KNIGHT, DIAN Kona
painting - watercolor
featured artist, 2nd edition

KOSADA, AN Kona
crafts - ceramics, fiber, paper

KOSKI, MARY Waimea
painting - oil
Choc Orch, Cunningham, Gal Gt Things, Isl Heritage

LA LONDE, ROBBI Puna
painting - watercolor
Gal Gt Things

LACY, MIKI Waimea
painting - watercolor
WAC

LAKE, TAI Kona
crafts - furniture
Fiberarts, Maya
featured artist, premiere & 2nd edition

LANG, SANDRA Puna
crafts - stained glass

LANG, STEPHEN Puna
crafts - lava rock, oil, photography

LANGE, SITA Puna
graphics - drawing, clay, mixed paints

LAWLESS, RICHARD Puna
sculpture

LE BUSE, MARK Hilo
crafts

LE BUSE, SUZZI Volcano
painting - oil, fabric

LEE, ELIZABETH Kona
crafts - lauhala weaving
featured artist, premiere & 2nd edition

LEE, GORDON Hilo
crafts - ceramics
featured artist, 2nd edition

LEMCKE, ANNE Kona
graphics-charcoal, oil

LEONE, DREW Hilo
painting - sculpture, mixed media
Gal Gt Things

LEONG, CHIU Volcano
crafts - ceramics
Gal Gt Things

LEWIS, BRAD Puna
photography
Choc Orch, Pahoa, VAC
featured artist, 2nd edition

LEWIS, JUNE Hilo
painting - watercolor

LEWIS, LAURA Hamakua
textiles - garment and interior designs
Fiberarts
featured artist, premiere edition

LIRETTE, LINDA Kona
painting - oil, watercolor, paper art

LONG, KATHY Waimea
graphics - pencil, oil, pastel
Choc Orch, Gal Gt Things
featured artist, premiere edition

LORENZEN, RICHARD Kona
crafts - bowl turning
VAC

LOYD, KATHY Hilo
painting - acrylic, mixed media
Loyd's

LOYD, KENNETH Hilo
painting - oil, serigraph, mixed media
Loyd's
featured artist, 2nd edition

LYONS, VONNIE Kona
painting - oils

MANHART, MARILYN Kona
painting

MARIE, SANDRA Kona
painting

MARKELL, MARK Volcano
photography

MARKELL, NALANI HUDDY Volcano
painting - watercolor
featured artist, 2nd edition

MARQUESS, GAYLE Kona
crafts - stained & beveled glass

MARSH, PATRICIA Kona
crafts - jewelry

MARSHALL, MICHAEL Hilo
sculpture

MARTIN, KOLEKA Waimea
textiles - fiber
Gal Gt Things

MASON, MILES Waimea
painting - watercolor
Choc Orch, Cunningham
featured artist, 2nd edition

MAUDSLEY WHITE, SHELLY Kona
painting - watercolor
Art Mart
featured artist, 2nd edition

McCARTY, CAROL Hilo
textiles - weaving
Gal Gt Things, VAC

McCORMICK, BETH Kona
crafts - featherwork
Choc Orch, Gal Gt Things, Showcase

McDONALD, MARIE Waimea
crafts - Hawaiian lei making
featured artist, premiere edition

McFAULL, FRAN Waimea
textiles - hand-painted hats
Fiberarts

McGRATH, PAMELA Kohala
textiles - silk painting

McGREGOR, DIANE Kona
painting - oil, pen & ink
featured artist, 2nd edition

McGUIRE, KEITH Kona
painting - watercolor
Choc Orch
featured artist, 2nd edition

McKENZIE, AMRTA Puna
graphics - drawing, clay, mixed paints

McLUCKIE, CHRIS Volcano
photography

McMILLEN, DIANE Kona
photography

MEDEIROS, EDWIN Kona
sculpture - wood
VAC
featured artist, 2nd edition

MEHAU, TOM Waimea
painting - watercolor, pen & ink drawing
WAC

MERCER, ROLAND Puna
painting - oil, gouache, etching

MEYERS-BEVERS, JILL AMI Kona
textiles - painting on silk

MILLAR, NINA Hamakua
textiles - handwoven clothing

MITCHELL, MEGAN Kona
photography - oils

MIYAMOTO, WAYNE Hilo
painting - oil, print making

MONTE, M Waimea
photography

MOON, JAN Hilo
textiles - fabric painting, pen & ink, pencil
Fiberarts
featured artist, 2nd edition

MOORE, DIANE Kona
crafts - basketry, fiber

MOREHOUSE, RANDY Puna
crafts - ceramics
Choc Orch, Gal Gt Things, Showcase
featured artist, 2nd edition

MORGAN, JAMES Kona
painting - watercolor
Choc Orch, Isl Heritage, Morgan/Reagan Arts
featured artist, premiere edition

MORINOUE, HIROKI Kona
painting - watercolor
Gal Gt Things

MORRISON, BOONE Volcano
photography
Gal Gt Things, VAC

MORRISS, LEX Waimea
crafts - ceramics
Waimea Gen St
featured artist, 2nd edition

MORTEMORE, RICHARD Hamakua
painting - watercolor
featured artist, 2nd edition

MOTTA, GORDON Hamakua
crafts - ceramics
Fiberarts
featured artist, premiere edition

MURPHY, GLENN Hilo
painting - watercolor, mixed media

NELSON, ERDINE Hilo
painting - watercolor, pastel, oil

NEWBERT, CHRIS Kona
photography
featured artist, premiere edition

NGUYEN BARKER, PHAN Kona
painting - batik painting on silk
Choc Orch, Cunningham, Multi-Arts, Showcase
featured artist, premiere edition

NICHOLS, ARLENE Kona
painting - wearable art, pastel, watercolor
KVA Gal, Showcase

NICHOLSON, EMERIC Kohala
painting - watercolor
Gal Gt Things, MKBH Gal

NIFASH, SACHI Kona
painting - oil

NIJENSOHN, JORGE Puna
painting - acrylic

NISHITA, KATHY Waimea
crafts - Hawaiian quilts

NOTT, CARTER Kona
crafts - jewelry

NOTTINGHAM HALVERSON, KARRON Hilo
textiles - weaving
featured artist, 2nd edition

NOVAK-NEAL, KARIN Kona
painting - watercolor, acrylic, mixed media
Choc Orch, Showcase

O'CONNOR, GWENDOLYN Puna
painting - watercolor on silk

O'FRIEL, NORA Puna
painting - painting on silk, garments
Gal Gt Things

O'NEILL, JAMES Kona
painting - oil

OBENCHAIN, DICK Hilo
painting - oil

OBERSOLER, SONIA Kona
crafts - Hawaiian quilts

ODA, AKI Hilo
crafts - ceramics

ODA, MAYUMI Kohala
painting
Gal Gt Things

OKANO, LAUREN Hilo
misc - caligraphy, mixed media
Okano Furniture
featured artist, premiere edition

ONO, IRA Volcano
textiles - wearable art, collage
VAC

OPENHEART, XO Puna
painting - oil
Pahoa

PAIVA, LILLIAN Hamakua
painting - pencil, oil, pen & ink

PALAKIKO, LEE Kona
photography
featured artist, premiere & 2nd edition

PALMER, SUZANNE Kohala
textiles - silk painting

PANIS, CLIFFORD Hilo
photography

PARENTE, STEVEN Hilo
painting - watercolor

PATTEN, DIVINA Kona
painting - oil, acrylic
Gal Gt Things

PAULL, AKEVA Kona
painting - watercolor, gouache, mixed media

PAUOLE, SUNNY Kona
painting - pastel, oil, air brush acrylic
Isl Heritage

PEIFER, DONNA Kona
painting - oil, pencil, graphics, watercolor

PELTON, RAYMOND Puna
sculpture - lava rock

PERRY, JAMIE Kona
crafts - sand painting
Fiberarts

PEZIM, SUSAN Kona
painting - acrylic, watercolor
Art Mart
featured artist, 2nd edition

PHREO, ZOE Puna
crafts - fiber

PONTIUS, GREG Kohala
sculpture - Hawaiian woods

PONTZ, JENNIFER Kona
crafts - etched glass
Choc Orch, Gal Gt Things, Showcase

POULOS, BETSY Puna
painting

POWER, LAURA Kohala
textiles - painting on silk
Gal Gt Things

POWERS, SUSAN Waimea
textiles - painting on silk
Gal Gt Things

PRATTAS, JAMES Kona
painting

PRICE, GLENNA Kohala
painting - watercolor, acrylic, oil, pastel

RANCHI, MAX Waimea
photography

RANKIN, PATRICK Kohala
painting
Gal Gt Things

RATHBUN, ANN Hilo
crafts - thrown porcelain

REED, MELISSA Hilo
painting - acrylic, mixed media

RICHARDSON, VIVIAN Hilo
Fiberarts

RILEY, MOMI Kona
crafts - Celtic harps, Grecian sun dials

RISSACHER, THOMAS Puna
painting - acrylic, oil stained & etched glass
Cunningham, VAC

ROBINSON, JAMES Hamakua
crafts - violins, bows, lutes

RODMAN, TERRIE Kona
crafts - weaving, fiber
featured artist, premiere & 2nd edition

ROEHRIG, ETHEL Hilo
painting - oil
Cunningham, VAC

ROLPH, DOROTHEA Kona
sculpture, watercolor

ROSE, MICHAEL Hamakua
painting - crylic

ROSEN, KAREN Kohala
textiles - painting on silk, wall hangings, garments
Gal Gt Things

ROSEN, SAM Kona
crafts - goldsmith, sculpture

RUDDLE, SHAY Hilo
painting - watercolor

RUSSELL, GEORGIA Hamakua
painting

RYCRAFT, KATHERINE Hilo
textiles - fabric design, batik, serigraph
Fiberarts

SALMOIRAGHI, FRANCO off-island
photography
Gal Gt Things, VAC
featured artist, premiere & 2nd edition

SAN MIGUEL, RICHARD Puna
graphics - graphic art

SAUNDERS, BARRY Kona
misc - video

SAXE, DOROTHY Kona
painting - oil

SCHULZE, SUSUN Waimea
painting - silk painting
Gal Gt Things

SERRAO, RICHARD Hilo
painting - acrylic, watercolor, drawing

SERVA, VICKI Kona
painting - watercolor, collage, formed paper
Choc Orch, Gal Gt Things, KVA Gal
featured artist, premiere & 2nd edition

SEXTON, LLOYD off-island
painting - oil
featured artist, 2nd edition

SHAPIRO, JOAN Kona
crafts - ceramics

SHAW, KRISTEN Kona
crafts - jewelry
Gal Gt Things

SHAZAR, E S Kona
painting - pastel, oil, watercolor

SHEELER, MICHAEL Kona
misc - film & computer animation, story board

SIGLER, EDWARD Kona
painting - oil

SLOTZKIN, ALEX Kona
crafts - jewelry
Gal Gt Things

SMOOT, BETTY Hilo
painting - oil portraits

SOGO, ROSETTA Puna
painting - watercolor, acrylic, mixed media

SORUM, JANET Kona
painting
Choc Orch, Cunningham, Gal Gt Things

SOUKOP, GARY Hamakua
crafts - furniture making
featured artist, 2nd edition

SPENCE, ROBERT Puna
painting - watercolor

STADLER, KATHERINE Hilo
crafts - ceramics

STAGNER, NORMAN Kona
painting - watercolor

StAMAND, LYNN Kona
painting - watercolor, woodcut, litho prints
Choc Orch, Multi-Arts
featured artist, premiere & 2nd edition

STARK, EMILY Kohala
painting - watercolor, acrylic, oil

STARR, KIM Kona
painting - oil
Choc Orch, Cunningham, Gal Gt Things

STEINER-JACKSON, SARA Puna
painting - watercolor, pen & ink, hand-colored prints
Gal Gt Things, Pahoa

STEINHILBER, BUDD Kona
painting - watercolor
Choc Orch, KVA Gal
featured artist, premiere edition

STERIOS, HOMER Puna
sculpture - bronze
featured artist, premiere edition

STEVENS, LINDA Puna
crafts - doll-making, watercolor
Choc Orch

STRAKA, JACK Puna
crafts - bowl turning
Gal Gt Things, Mart & MacA

SUFRIN, ALICE Kona
painting - collage, sculpture, stage & costume

SUMNER, ERIC Puna
painting - oil

SWERDLOW, SUE Waimea
painting - watercolor, acrylic, graphics
Choc Orch, Gal Gt Things, VAC
featured artist, premiere edition

TAHLMAN, HAP Kohala
crafts - furniture
Gal Gt Things

TAKAKI, RANDALL Puna
sculpture

TANIMOTO, LYNN Hilo
photography

TARLETON, DAVID Waimea
crafts - bowl turning
Gal Gt Things, Mart & MacA

TAUBE, TERRY Kona
crafts - paper making

TELEA, LAWRENCE Puna
painting - air brush, printmaking

THANOS, DIANA Kona
painting - Choc Orch

THOMAS, JOHN Kona
painting - oil, watercolor, graphics
Choc Orch, Cunningham, Isl Heritage, Malama, Maya, MKBH Gal, VAC
featured artist, premiere & 2nd edition
cover artist, premiere edition

THOMAS, LEE ALLEN Kohala
photography
Choc Orch

THOMAS, TERRY Puna
crafts - ceramics

THOMPSON, DOUGLAS Hilo
painting - oil, gouache, watercolor, pen & ink

THRASHER, KAREN Waimea
crafts - stained glass, acrylic, pencil
VAC

THRASHER, MOSES Waimea
crafts - jewelry

THRELFALL, JOHN Volcano
crafts - cermaics
Gal Gt Things

THURSTON, SHINDRU Hamakua
crafts - eramics

TIMBOY, MARCIA Hilo
painting - mixed media

TOMONO, BARBARA Volcano
textiles - trad Japanese dyes, fabrics
Fiberarts

TOMONO, LONNY Volcano
crafts - trad Japanese woodworking, sculpture, furniture
featured artist, 2nd edition

TREDWAY, CAROL Kona
painting - watercolor, oil, acrylic

TRUMAN, REBECCA Hilo
sculpture - clay, bronze, oil, watercolor

VAN ASPEREN HUME, PATRICIA Kona
crafts - etched & stained glass

VAN DER HORST, ROZEMARYN Kona
painting - watercolor, drawing

VAN LOON, ROLAND Puna
painting

VANDERSCHOOT, ARI off-island
painting - oil
featured artist, premiere edition

VAREZ, DIETRICH Volcano
graphics - prints
Cunningham, VAC

VAREZ, LINDA Volcano
painting
VAC

VAUGHN, DAVID Hilo
painting - oil, acrylic, pen & ink, graphics

VIGNATO, WARREN Kohala
sculpture

VOGEL, SONJA Kau
painting - oil, textiles, mixed media
VAC

WAGNER, GARY Kohala
crafts - etched glass
Gal Gt Things

WALKER, BONITA Kona
textiles - wearable art, mixed media, acrylic

WARNER, JAY Puna
crafts - wood working
Gal Gt Things, Mart & MacA

WARNER, TERRY Hilo
photography

WARSHAUER, KENT Volcano
sculpture - welded steel, mixed media
VAC

WATT, NORMA Puna
painting - watercolor

WAYMOUTH, FLEUR Kona
photography
Gal Gt Things

WEBB, JOANN Puna
crafts - weaving

WEISEL, DORIAN Volcano
photography
Gal Gt Things

WEST, J JAY Waimea
crafts - fiber, mixed media graphics
Aries Graphics

WEST, SUZANE Waimea
crafts
fiber, clay

WEYHREN, RIXANNE Kona
photography
Fiberarts

WILLIAMS, CHARLOTTE Hilo
textiles - fiber, weaving
the Center

WILLIAMS, DOROTHY off-island
painting - oil, acrylic
featured artist, premiere edition

WILLIAMS, GLENN Kona
crafts - bowls, wood working
Gal Gt Things, Mart & MacA

WILLIS, JOAN Hilo
crafts - ceramics, porcelain, acrylic

WILSON, ALEXIS Kona
painting - watercolor, pencil, pen & ink
Choc Orch

WILSON, JANE Kona
painting - watercolor
KVA Gal
featured artist, premiere edition

WILSON, NORMA Kona
painting - oil
KVA Gal
featured artist, premiere edition

WISHARD, HARRY Waimea
painting - oil, pencil, collage
Gal Gt Things
featured artist, premiere & 2nd edition

WOLD, MARILYN off-island
crafts - paper making
featured artist, premiere edition

WOO, ERNA Puna
painting - mixed media
Pahoa

WOOD, ELDON Hilo
crafts - glass

WOODWELL, ALDEN Kona
painting - oil

WORLEY, ROBIN Hilo
painting - painting on silk, watercolor

WRIGHT, JON Hamakua
painting - acrylic
VAC

YAMAZAWA, WILFRED Kona
crafts - glass blowing
Isl Heritage, VAC
featured artist, premiere & 2nd edition

YOKOYAMA, KAY Hilo
painting - oil, graphics, doll making

ZANE, SIG Hilo
textiles - fabric design, clothing design
Sig Zane Designs

ZUFICH, NANCY Kona
painting - acrylic trompe l'oeil, watercolor
Choc Orch, KVA Gal

ZUKE, BILL Kona
painting

INDEX

Aanavi, Don 73
Ad Studio Kona 13, 62, 68, 77
Advertiser, The Honolulu 13, 20-21, 36-37, 69, 76
Ahia, Christine 63, 65
Ahlo & Associates Inc. 113
Akiona, Christy 6, 29
Alexander, Garron 61, 65
Alfredo's Photo Studio 13, 47, 57, 66, 76
Althouse, Robert 103
Anbe, Takashi 97
Anderson, David 9, 45, 69
Art Mart of Kona 13, 58, 64, 67, 69, 72
Au Hoy, Fanny Collins 106

Balai, Sharon 53, 65
Banks, Ken 94-95
Berger-Mahoney, Marian 51, 65
Big Island Group 112
Blackwell Custom Furniture 13, 48, 65, 71
Blackwell, Peter 48, 65
Bonk, Fumie cover, inside front flap, 9, 84
Bradley Properties, Ltd. 13, 26-27, 69, 71
Breese Rabin, Teunisse 60, 65
Bruno, Leon 99

C. J. Kimberly Realtors 13, 43, 67, 73
Campbell, John 101
Capricorn Bookshop 107
Carrington, Kent 102
Center, The 100, 114
Chao, Linus 24, 32-33, 65, 96-97
Chocolate Orchid Gallery 89, 114
Clark, Lisa 13, 62, 66, 112
Clark, Putman 13, 46, 47, 112
Clemmer & Clemmer 110
Coburn, Janet L. 6
Colors of Hawaii 109
Contemporary Museum 76
Cottage Gallery 105, 114
Crockett, Rebecca 6, 9, 78-83
Cunningham Gallery 111

DeLuz, Dan 34-35, 65
Destination Hilo 113
Destination: Kona Coast 113

Family Crisis Shelter 112
Fiberarts/Topstitch 13, 49, 68, 71
Forcier, Audrey 101
Franzen, David 73
Freed, Ray 8, 12
Friends of Garron Alexander 13, 61, 65, 72
Fry, Miles 81
Fujii, Jocelyn 20-21
Furelos, Alfredo 18, 22, 26, 30, 36, 42, 45-46, 48-50, 54-58, 61-63, 66-69, 76, 81, 84-85

Gallery of Great Things 91, 114
Gardner, Barbara 59, 66
Gomes, David 18-19, 66
Greenwell, Mary Emily Sexton 16-17
Gross, Ed 58, 59, 64

Hawaii Preparatory Academy 112
Hawaii Tribune-Herald 13, 58, 68, 74
Hawaii Trop. Botanical Garden 108
Hennes, Joanne 52, 66
Henry Opukahaia School 112
Hess, Harvey 8
Hilo Accident ... Clinic 13, 28-29, 68, 70
Holualoa Management Company 13, 51, 65, 75
HPM Building Supply 13, 55, 69, 75
Hulihe'e Palace Museum 80, 82, 106, 114

Iijima, Renee 20
Insurance Hawaii 110
Island Heritage Collection 90, 114
Izumi, Jason 30-31, 66

Jardine, William and Kathleen 13, 63, 69, 111

Kahilu Theatre 104, 114
Kaiama, Tsugi 22-23, 66
Kailua Village Artists Gallery 92, 114
Kanouff, J. Michael 53
Kasser, Mike and Beth 13, 51, 65, 110
Kayton, Edwin 60, 66
Keauhou Beach Hotel 13, 47, 69, 72
Keauhou Village Book Shop 13, 60, 65, 77
Keauhou-Kona Realty, Inc. 13, 60, 65, 72
Kim, Millicent 11
Knight, Dian 62, 66
Kodama, Paul 29
Kohler, Adi 14
Kona Family YMCA 110
Kona Historical Society 113
Kona Ranch House 13, 52, 66, 77

Lake, Tai 56, 66
Lanihau Center 13, 22-23, 66, 70
Lassiter, Pudding 83, 98
Lee, Elizabeth 59, 66-67
Lee, Gordon 24-25, 67
Lewis, Brad 41, 67
Lewis, Laura 6
Loyd's Art Supply 13, 44, 67, 75
Loyd, Kenneth 44, 67
Lyman House Memorial Museum 99, 114

Makio, Norman 34, 44, 55, 83
Malama Arts Inc. 13, 34-35, 65, 72, 113
Markell, Kai III 13, 64, 67, 112
Markell, Nalani Huddy 64, 67
Marshall, Michael 94
Martin & MacArthur 109
Maryl Development 13, 54, 69, 75
Mason, Miles 46, 67
Maudsley White, Shelly 64, 67
Mauna Kea Beach Hotel 13, 14-17, 73
Mauna Lani Resort, Inc. 13, 18-19, 30-31, 66, 74
Mauna Loa Macadamia Nuts 111
Maya Gallery inside front flap, 87, 114
McGregor, Diane 43, 67
McGuire, Keith 62, 68
McMillen, Diane 60
Meadow Gold Dairies 13, 63, 65, 71
Medeiros, Edwin 42, 68
Mehle, Leila 100
Modern Camera 51
Moon, Jan 49, 68
Morehouse, Randy 58, 68
Morriss, Lex 61, 68
Mortemore, Richard 50, 68
Multi-Arts Incorporated 13, 40, 69, 75, 111

Ng, Gordon 17
Nguyen Barker, Phan 75
North Hawaii Community Hospital 111
Nottingham Halverson, Karron 28-29, 68
Noyle, Rick 59

Orchid Isle Auto Center 13, 50, 68, 74

Pahoa Arts and Crafts Guild 102, 114
Palakiko, Lee 47, 69, 107
Peggy Chesnut & Company 13, 56, 66, 73
Personal Business Manager 13, 42, 68, 71
Pezim, Susan 58, 69
Pfaff, Virginia 104
Phyllis Sellens and Company 13, 38-39, 69, 77

Rainbow Advertising, 110
Reyn Spooner Inc. 13, 59, 66, 76
Rodman, Terrie 9, 38-39, 69
Roussell's 108

Salmoiraghi, Franco 20-21, 69
Serva, Vicki 54, 69
Sexton, Lloyd 8, 14-17, 69, 73
Sherrard, Frances 100
Showcase Gallery 88, 114
Smart, Richard 104
Soukup, Gary 9, 45, 69
StAmand, Lynn 40, 69, 75

Tanner, Jerré Music Studio 110
Tanner, Jerré E. 8-9, 38-39, 75, inside back flap
Thomas, John 6, 26-27, 69, 85
Thomas, Lee 26, 38-39
Tomono, Barbara 55
Tomono, Lonny 55, 69
Tropical Dreams 108

University of Hawaii Hilo 8, 13, 24-25, 32-33, 65, 67, 70, 94-97
UpCountry Quilters 13, 53, 65, 73

Valley Interiors 112
Volcano Art Center 101, 114

Waihe'e, John 10, 81
Wailoa Center 98, 114
Waimea Art Center 103, 114
Waimea General Stone 13, 61, 68, 77
Weeks, Henry 9, 79-83, 106
West Hawaii Arts Guild 107, 113
West Hawaii Gallery 107, 114
Winkler Wood Products, Inc. 13, 45, 69, 76
Wishard, Harry 63, 69

Yamazawa, Wilfred 36-37, 69

The Second Edition has been made on the Island of Hawaii using an Amiga 1000 computer with Professional Page software by Gold Disk Inc., a QMS-PS 810 PostScript laser printer for layout and text proofs, typesetting in Adobe Optima fonts by Photocomp R B Ltd. in Montreal, Canada, and printed by Golden Cup Printing Company Ltd. in British Hong Kong.